T0246655

PRAISE FOR JEFF ENGLE AND

ALL THE WAR THEY WANT

"For Jeff's entire career, he has been working on the most difficult and important problems affecting our country with a high degree of success. He has the traits (intelligence, grit, determination) that only the elite of the elite have. The concepts and the approach that he has learned through practical experience are the only way to solve the difficult challenges our country is facing in the cybersecurity arena."

—**Gerard Amaro,** Executive Director and
Chief Revenue Officer, Conquest Cyber

"*All the War They Want* is a hard-hitting sharing of Jeff's experiences and lessons learned in combat, business, and life. It's an opportunity for the reader to see unconventional techniques for looking at problems and use them to overcome challenges in life and business."

—**Rich Robertson,** U.S. Special Operations Command
Program Manager, Oak Ridge National Laboratory

"I came to learn by observing Jeff; he will achieve any outcome he sets his mind to achieve. When he told me he would build a company that would function as an elite, high-performing team, I knew I wanted to be a part of it. His ability to vision, combined with his willingness to take risks and nontraditional approaches, makes him a formidable business leader, capable of building a world-class elite organization."

—**Sarah Nurse,** Senior Vice President
of Operations, Conquest Cyber

"Jeff is constantly on the search to make a difference in the world and make his mark. Little to no other people exist of his caliber—he is an irreplaceable asset in more ways than one."

—**Christen Prasse,** Head of Strategic
Accounts, Conquest Cyber

"It is evident from the moment you hear Jeff speak that his life's work is freedom. He understands the world on a macro and micro level, and his contribution to the world is limitless."

—**Elizabeth Goodwin,** Managing Director, CBRE

"I have never met anyone like Jeff. He is a true inspiration to do the most in life and to conquer any situation with a lighthearted and strategic approach. He is a leader in every respect. He challenges your way of thinking and gives you the confidence you need to succeed."

—**Jody Perez,** Marketing Lead, Conquest Cyber

"Jeff's superpower is breaking people out of their comfort zones. By nature, he is an unconventional leader who refuses to follow the way of the world. His demeanor makes those around him want to do better, be better, and fight harder."

—**Carmen Brooks,** Executive Operations
Manager, Conquest Cyber

"Jeff Engle is a member of a rare breed of warrior-poets, whose dedication and conviction to the fight for our nation and our way of life have manifested in various capacities in his lifetime of service: special operator, biochemical emergency expert, and now, cybersecurity thought leader and innovator. It does not take long for anyone who has met Jeff in person to realize and imagine the level of conviction and mental focus that he has put into honing his mind and his craft to produce the ideas, beliefs, and actions needed to execute and win on this new cybersecurity battlefield. The principles and alternative thinking that he espouses in *All the War They Want* are not abstract or merely theoretical—they have been hardened and tested by Jeff and others in the crucible of combat, both in the physical and cyber war zones. Could not be prouder of him."

—**Doug Kim,** Senior Vice President of
Cyber Risk, Conquest Cyber

JEFFREY J. ENGLE

ALL
THE
WAR
THEY
WANT

Special Operations Techniques for
Winning in Cyber Warfare, Business, and Life

GREENLEAF
BOOK GROUP PRESS

Published by Greenleaf Book Group Press
Austin, Texas
www.gbgpress.com

Distributed by Greenleaf Book Group

For ordering information or special discounts for bulk purchases, please contact Greenleaf Book Group at PO Box 91869, Austin, TX 78709, 512.891.6100.

Design and composition by Greenleaf Book Group and Teresa Muniz
Cover design by Greenleaf Book Group and Teresa Muniz
Cover images used under license from ©Shutterstock/CoreDESIGN. Security icon from ©The Noun Project/Iconographer

Publisher's Cataloging-in-Publication data is available.

Print ISBN: 978-1-62634-972-8

eBook ISBN: 978-1-62634-973-5

Part of the Tree Neutral® program, which offsets the number of trees consumed in the production and printing of this book by taking proactive steps, such as planting trees in direct proportion to the number of trees used: www.treeneutral.com

Printed in the United States of America on acid-free paper

22 23 24 25 26 27 28 29   10 9 8 7 6 5 4 3 2 1

First Edition

For the tiny fraternity whose common bond is uncommon valor.
Most owe you more than they will ever know.
I owe you it all.

Fighting is foundational to the human spirit. For millennia, we woke up every day fighting to survive; we built bonds with the people to our left and right that are stronger than blood—on par with or exceeding faith. We found purpose and focus that built societies and ways of life. Always striving for progress. Yes, fighting can be brutal, but the willingness to fight can also prevent brutality. It can destroy, yet it can be a catalyst for growth. It is at that sad moment when people no longer have something to fight for that hope is lost.

CONTENTS

FOREWORD

've spent over thirty years in the technology industry, most recently
as president and CEO of Citrix Systems, leading a global team of ten
thousand. Tech is a fascinating business because of its transformative
pace and pervasive influence on society. However, running a large organization is all consuming and leaves little opportunity to pursue personal
passions—in my case, things like adventure travel, flying, and golf.

Speaking of golf, a few years ago I was asked to sponsor a golf tournament
in support of special operations veterans and in recognition of the lasting
health impact that many of them experience from years of training and
combat. Combining my favorite sport and a great cause was a no-brainer.
Jeff Engle joined our foursome on tournament day as a representative of the
special ops community, having served as the youngest-ever member of his
special missions unit, arguably the military's most elite. Unfortunately, he
was unable to play—and, frankly, barely able to walk—because of a surgery
he'd had just days earlier to repair old injuries. I was immediately struck by
Jeff's grit and commitment to the cause as he spent the day engaging with
my team from Citrix despite what I imagine was debilitating pain. His
quiet, humble, and thoughtful approach was so different from the typical
Hollywood portrayal of a special operations warrior.

Since our first meeting, Jeff has been quite busy building a rapidly
growing company in the most dynamic and critical part of the technology

landscape—cybersecurity. Over the past few years, he and I have had the chance to golf, fish, and just talk about life and business, finding many common interests both personally and professionally. One common thread has been the critical importance and challenges of building and leading successful teams, whether in the military, the public sector, or the private sector. People are an organization's most valuable asset and the foundation for building sustainable value. How teams are built and led is not a science but an art based on personal experiences. After watching how Jeff has built and led his team, inspired by his service in special ops—and how he strives to rally all of us to his critical cause of defending America in cyberspace—I believe him to be an artist of the highest order. Unconventional, creative, a rule breaker in the best sense of the term—that's Jeff Engle. He's the kind of forward-thinking problem solver we business leaders would do well to emulate in this dynamic tech-driven age.

That's why this book is so timely and important, and it is why Jeff was the perfect person to write it. He has fashioned a modern, counterintuitive, highly effective leadership formula that gets results—even when the business battlefield is littered with land mines and attacks are incoming from all directions.

We very much need Jeff's fresh approach to team building and management right now. Think about it: Today's conventional corporate management theory was constructed on a practical basis from lessons learned by the military during World War II, leading to a command-and-control hierarchy for coordination across large, distributed organizations. Strategy and objectives are defined at the top of the pyramid, while tasks are cascaded down through the levels to be implemented according to established policy. The model, though proven to scale throughout the twentieth century, is slow and unempowering for most.

We've moved beyond that now. The incredible era in which we live is often described as the Imagination Age, characterized by the interconnection of systems and devices, the transparency of information, artificial intelligence, and other innovations. In theory, technology should now augment human capabilities to achieve an unprecedented increase in prosperity and output, but that is not what always happens. For example, corporate productivity in the aggregate has been decelerating for years. At the same time, technology is challenging the benefits of scale and the traditional command-and-control structure, thus reducing barriers to entry, changing the nature of competition, and posing entirely new challenges to our economic, physical, and digital security. Addressing these threats requires us to consider a new operating model for future competitiveness.

That's where Jeff comes in. As I read this book, I was intrigued by how he uses a window into the current cyber warfare landscape, as well as his own experiences as a special operator, to outline a modern, practical formula for management and organizational success. In the special ops world in which he used to function, failure to execute could be fatal. In the cyber realm in which he operates today, failure to execute isn't measured as a customer who is temporarily disappointed but rather one who may be facing an existential threat to their business. Thus, he is uniquely qualified to define and champion a model for how the most impactful teams can be built, organized, and engaged. His conclusions are born from real-life combat experience, not simple theory.

Cyber is one of the very few industries in which military analogies are completely appropriate. The war is real, the stakes are incredibly high, and we are arguably in danger of losing. As Jeff says, for many of our adversaries, "hacking" is just a business—a business unconstrained by traditional rules or regulations. Defending and winning in the cyber arena requires an approach with unprecedented speed and flexibility, which is unnatural for most organizations. Yet knowing what it takes to redefine the rules and challenge conventional wisdom to ensure success is applicable across almost every industry and business.

Business leaders today are fighting a war across multiple fronts: for talent, customers, market share, and so many other resources. Most will lose if they fail to assemble the right team. How the team is selected—and how it operates as a unit—will define the outcome of the organization. When properly deployed, this process becomes an organization's enduring culture, allowing the system to expand and succeed beyond the influence of any single leader.

All the War They Want demonstrates this approach in action, from the physical battlefield to the wars being fought in the virtual world. Jeff illustrates how unconventional, elite organizations are built through a rigorous self-selection process, how leaders can enable versus merely manage, and how the most powerful accountability is *cultural*—because it is voluntary, proactive, and based on heart. As Jeff so eloquently explains in the pages ahead, *when your team knows that they are doing cool stuff that makes an impact alongside people they like, then you will have created an unstoppable force.*

I was honored and humbled when Jeff asked me to write the foreword to this book. He has made such significant contributions to our country with his military service and now on the front lines of the next frontier as CEO of a rapidly growing cybersecurity company protecting our nation's critical infrastructure. He's a true American success story and an exceptional leader whose example we ought to follow, not only as we seek to build our elite business teams but also as we fight together in cyberspace to protect the American way of life. I can't imagine anyone with whom I would rather be in the trenches. By the time you finish reading this book, I am confident that you will feel the same way.

David Henshall
Former president and CEO of Citrix Systems

INTRODUCTION

War is the remedy that our enemies have chosen,
and I say let us give them all they want.

—Attributed to **William Tecumseh Sherman**

APRIL 9, 2004, BAGHDAD

It was well after sunset, and I was getting ready to head out on patrol projecting from an armored personnel carrier, known as a Bradley, with a .50 caliber machine gun up top. I was a young sergeant in the 1st Cavalry Division on my third deployment in Iraq, stationed at Forward Operating Base (FOB) Falcon on the southern edge of Baghdad. My platoon's mission that night was to do route clearance, an innocuous way of saying that we would be driving up and down the roads waiting to get hit by IEDs (improvised explosive devices) so the convoys behind us could come through safely. Not a very sexy assignment. As we geared up and planned the route, the chorus to the battle hymn of the Airborne, "Blood on the Risers," played on repeat in my head: *Gory, gory, what a hell of a way to die.*

I would have sworn it was "glory," but at the time I did not realize the implications of the tune or the correct wording. "Blood on the Risers" is intended to be a cautionary tale of how doing everything right, except one crucial thing, can be disastrous. As the story goes, this rookie paratrooper shook with fright, did everything right, but forgot to hook up his static line, the mechanism that automatically opens the main parachute as paratroopers exit the door (or ramp) of the plane. If you fail to "hook up," then you have to revert to your reserve, and, as in the case of the protagonist in the song, your probability of having a particularly bad outcome is increased.

Which leads me to the three principles that are repeated throughout this book:

1. People don't rise to the level of their potential; they fall to the level of their training.

2. If it is important, then you test it—frequently.

3. If a predictable response can be evoked, it can be exploited.

I was serving as the assistant patrol leader that night in Baghdad. My lieutenant was in the lead vehicle, and I was on the armored personnel carrier manning the .50 cal., bringing up the rear of our string of three vehicles carrying around fifteen people. Since the lieutenant and I were going over the route, our drivers were tasked with checking communications and mounting the guns. As we rolled out onto Route Irish and made the turn onto Route Senators, we discovered that I was the only one with the ability to contact the Company Tactical Operations Center (TOC) because my patrol leader had lost communications (or potentially never had it). I was all of twenty-years old, yet I was the most combat-tested member of my platoon, having already served two tours and now a few weeks into my third.

This was during the Mahdi uprising when Iraq was transitioning from post-invasion to insurgency by various groups, including Shia militias aligned with Muqtada al-Sadr, a radical cleric leading the opposition to foreign presence in the region. It was an extremely dicey time for everyone on the ground. With each passing deployment I had noticed that the rules of engagement had become more and more constraining. It was as if the enemy was evolving, and we were devolving into having fewer tools at our disposal from an operational standpoint. On this particular day, we'd received intelligence that al-Sadr's militia planned to be very active that night, making trouble for carnival game patrols like ours. What form that trouble might take and when it might occur were a mystery. The only thing we knew for certain was that we were the primary—and slow-moving—targets. This was due to the purely reactive nature of conventional forces at the time.

We were rumbling along doing our route clearance when we were ordered to stop driving because no convoys would be coming down our road for a while. We ended up parked on a bridge overlooking a major thoroughfare called Route Senators. It was a beautiful night, eerily quiet and pitch black. From my perch behind the .50 cal., I watched a long convoy of the 1st Armored Division coming out of the Green Zone—the heavily-fortified area of central Baghdad—and heading south toward our position. This was the unit we had done the "left seat/right seat" rides with as we replaced them. "Left seat/right seat" is a military term for describing the transitioning of mission or battlespace responsibility from one unit to another, in which you initially "shadow" the departing unit as they conduct operations and later take the lead with a select cadre of the previous unit as support and guidance prior to their complete departure (and presumable return home).

There were about twenty vehicles including armored Humvees and Bradley fighting vehicles in the battle space. These folks had been in Iraq for a year already and right before they were set to go home, they received the crushing news that their deployment had been extended. On this night they were headed to their new home base for the remainder of their tour. *Poor bastards*, I thought as I watched them stream past. *They were so close to getting out.*

And that's when the first IED blast hit. As I looked on from a distance, the 1st Armored Division convoy was attacked from the south by IEDs, rocket-propelled grenades (RPGs), and small arms fire. One IED disabled a Bradley and, as we found out later, killed some members of the crew. The Bradleys and the gunners on the Humvees engaged, and tracer fire sprayed across the southern horizon in the direction of some old apartment buildings—it was more suppressive fire rather than shooting at an identifiable and targeted enemy. This was the same spot where we had been hit a few days prior. An RPG struck one of our vehicles and caught one of my soldiers on fire when it struck the rear door jamb of the Up-Armored Humvee.

We had to get out of there, but our normal route back to the base would lead us straight into the carnage that had just befallen the 1st Armored. I called the lieutenant on the radio, and we decided to use Route Sonics to cut across to Route Irish, the road that would take us back to FOB Falcon. We started moving out but just as my vehicle got about a quarter mile into Route Sonics all the streetlights suddenly cut out. I spun the turret to the right and there was an explosion to my left. Deafening noise. Shrapnel flying. The clanging sound of it pelting our vehicles. I was hit in the left eye with shrapnel, my goggles blown off, my jaw fractured. I spun back around to the left and saw an RPG skip in front of the lieutenant's Humvee. Machine gun fire was coming in from two different positions now. Immediately, I ordered the others to get down and moved to lay down suppressive fire, but my .50 cal. jammed.

If I didn't get that gun functioning in a hurry, I would have no way to provide cover for my platoon or defend myself. The only way to fix it, however, was to get on top of the gun and remove the jam, exposing

HEADSPACE AND TIMING

Headspace and timing are measurements required to ensure the proper functioning of the .50 caliber machine gun. When headspace and timing are off, the gun is going to jam, a situation that is all too common. It is also a euphemism for someone who is screwing up or "not firing on all cylinders."

myself to incoming fire with zero protection. I didn't hesitate. As I climbed on top of the turret to remove the jam, I simultaneously called the lieutenant's vehicle.

There's an important tactical thing to understand about such combat situations. In the army we are taught that the best response to an ambush is to put your head down and get off the "X"—drive straight through the ambush zone as fast as you can so that you are harder to hit. Whatever you do, *don't stop*. That is the conventional wisdom, and that is what we were trained to do. It was drilled into our heads over and over again, with the goal of that reaction becoming so deeply ingrained that we wouldn't have to think twice in an emergency. We would just do it instinctively, immediately enacting the evoked response. It is not hyperbole when I say that evoked responses have been the cause of some of the greatest victories and worst defeats in human history.

However, perched on top of that turret with live fire all around, unable to see out of one eye, I decided *to hell with my training*, to hell with the conventional wisdom of driving through ambushes. I called the lieutenant's vehicle and told him to turn around, and I had my driver stay in place so we could lay down suppressive fire while they got out of the kill zone.

"I'm hit," I said calmly over the whir of the engines and the piercing sound of machine gun fire. "We've gotta get to the Green Zone. Turn around, and I'll cover you!"

As bullets walked up the side of the vehicle toward me, I fixed my jammed machine gun while my driver positioned us between the enemy and our escaping patrol. Led by the lieutenant's Humvee, the patrol streamed past me making a dash for the safety of the Green Zone about a quarter mile away. I had my driver do a pivot steer—a fast 180-degree turn—spinning my turret in the direction of the incoming fire. As we spun around, the enemy was once again walking 7.62 mm rounds up the side of the vehicle toward me. Once my patrol was headed toward the Green Zone, I took up the rear position and followed them, returning fire to cover their backs as we raced away.

I would spend the next several hours in the 31st Combat Support Hospital with a team of doctors trying to save my eye. Thankfully, they were successful. But in the bed next to me was a young private with his guts on his chest. My greatest concern at that moment was the lack of focus on him as they worked to save my eye. A piece of shrapnel had sliced his stomach open. They had pulled out some of his internal organs to identify any lacerations so that they did not make the mistake of closing him up with an internal bleed. Lying on his back, guts on his chest, and tortured by the urge to urinate, his greatest concern was the attractive nurse who would not leave the room so he could piss into the container she provided. Embarrassment is a powerful thing.

Half of my platoon would end up being wounded that month. All around me, good people—people who were trying to do the right thing for our country and the world—were losing: losing limbs, losing lives, losing the fight. Most of them had no business being there. They had joined for the college money or just to escape from their sleepy little hometowns. Some of them, though, were true warriors whose abilities were being wasted—driving up and down the roads waiting to get hit, only to be medevaced back to base, where they would weld more metal onto their Humvees and go back out on patrol.

There is no nobility in accepting defeat.

That is how I viewed the mission. Defeat.

At that point, I did not really see a lot of value in what we were doing. My opinion was confirmed when I found out that Route Sonics, just beyond the point where I had ordered my platoon to stop and turn around on the night of our ambush, had been daisy-chained with IEDs by insurgents. Had we followed the rules and continued down that road, there is no doubt in my mind that I, being fully exposed on the turret with no armor to protect me, would have died along with multiple others in my platoon.

If my brush with death on April 9, 2004—my Alive Day, as we say in the military—taught me anything, it is that if you really want to overcome a grave challenge, whether it's in war, business, or any other aspect of life, you have to be prepared to do whatever it takes to win. Even if that means breaking the rules, and damned what anyone thinks about it.

Making that split-second decision based off what I was seeing on the battlefield and in direct opposition to my training not only spared my life but earned me an Army Commendation for Valor in addition to the Purple Heart. It also helped me earn an invitation to try out for the most elite special operations organization in the world, where I was privileged to become one of the youngest members in history. This would be where I spent my formative years, surrounded by the most inspiring and dynamic people on the planet, and together, taking on the highest-value targets in the "war against terror." My time in special operations served as a stark contrast to the other experiences I'd had spanning from early childhood into my twenties, which largely stood to illuminate what *not* to do. In special operations, I saw time and again the value of violating the rules of convention—not in a fumbling, haphazard, rebel-without-a-cause way, but in a logical, tactical, and creative way that allowed us to fully explore the art of the possible and create a competitive advantage even when the deck was stacked against us.

Sadly, my time in special operations came to an end at the close of 2009, when I was forced to assume a quasi-military civilian role for the next three years while my medical retirement was processed. But that did not mean I was done fighting. These days I'm on a different mission, one that's just as critical to protecting our American way of life as was my time in special ops: marshalling the collective resources to address America's most pressing national security challenge, the war in cyberspace—the Fifth Domain.

For those reasons, when I was given the opportunity to take the reins, I was determined to do it differently. That is why I run my companies using the lessons I learned in the special operations community—the only place I have seen it done right. Since the inception, we have been going against the grain of convention while achieving an outsized impact. Racing to create a competitive advantage for our country's critical infrastructure sectors in a war that most Americans do not even realize they are fighting. Alternatively, the other side is focused, sophisticated, highly determined, and working perpetually to degrade and undermine our national security.

THE SPECIAL OPS APPROACH TO PROBLEM SOLVING

There is a war raging against our way of life, and it is an existential threat. Because it is taking place in cyberspace (what has come to be called the Fifth Domain), the majority of people do not recognize much of what is happening, and what *is* widely known is not taken seriously enough. Every network is quite literally under attack; every email provider, cloud provider, cybersecurity company, public utility, and government agency is under constant assault. Some of the attackers are from other countries, some are members of criminal gangs, and many others are just recklessly curious about whether or not they can succeed at hacking into a system. Who is attacking is almost less relevant than the fact that we are under attack constantly, and our adversaries are doing whatever they can to figure out what means of infiltration will work. Meanwhile, we are playing a lame form of defense based on conventional wisdom, and it goes something like this: if there is a talent gap in the cybersecurity arena (which there is, and a massive one at that) you add talent. If something is unsecured, you secure it. If something is not patched, you patch it. What that reactive and predictable response fails to recognize is that there is no such thing as a checklist approach to winning in war, and make no mistake, we are at war in cyberspace. We are building six-foot fences, they are building seven-foot ladders. As soon as we discover that they have breached our fence, we add two feet to the top. The adversary builds a taller ladder. Rinse and repeat. That is the conventional way to fight back, and it has been America's response to cyber warfare thus far. It is not working. We are in danger of losing this fight and our place in this world. Our way of life is hanging in the balance.

That is why I am advocating a different approach to problem solving—an approach grounded in those special operations principles that I embraced in my formative years. It started two decades ago with my work finding and eliminating weapons of mass destruction (WMDs), fighting terrorism, and battling global infectious disease, and is now squarely focused on the conflict taking place in cyberspace. There has not been a day in the past twenty years dealing with these existential threats to our way of life that I had to rely on habit, discipline, motivational memes, or the outside world to inspire me to act. I think in terms of risk—what is important to me, what could hurt it, and what mechanisms are in place that might enable the negative outcome. In light of those variables, my focus is honed. My passion ignited.

This is not about me, though. It is about applying the formula rooted in a cause that inspires you and getting the problem solved. It is about creating an elite team, expanding that team's capabilities outward, and creating a movement that is bigger than you can ever control. A movement that recognizes the value and importance of the cause and ignites the right kind of passion and grit—especially when there are insidious forces against you and tangible feedback or positive reinforcement is lacking. Success goes unacknowledged and failures are debilitating, if not disastrous. These kinds of missions are not for the faint of heart, and that is why they require special operations principles and an asymmetric approach to stack the deck in your favor.

First, you have to realize any challenge—including cyber warfare—is just a game. You can choose to play or not. Either way, there are going to be consequences. In cyber warfare, all of us (except the freakish few who live in the middle of nowhere with tin foil hats) have chosen to play but refuse to acknowledge that it is a game or admonish those who would use that terminology associated with war because of the seriousness. Of those who implicitly acknowledge it is a game, the majority refuse to play to win, whether they realize it or not. Instead, they follow perceived or established rules, believing themselves a pawn or, at best, a mere modestly powerful rook on this 3D chess board, limited in their capacity and awaiting guidance from someone else who, theoretically, must have a master plan. But who? Government? Elon Musk? Bill Gates?

Here's a bit of insight from having been at the table for incredibly consequential scenarios that required some major problem solving: no one is going to save you. You need to go figure it out. If you are fine with being in the matrix, be in the matrix. If you are going to do something about pollution in the oceans, a terror organization on the rise, or, in my case, the creeping infiltration into our vital technological nervous system, you need to change the way you think.

And that begins with having a fundamental understanding and acceptance of all the norms and conventions, and then recognizing that just because they are the current standard operating procedure, does not mean they are the only way. *We don't have to be beholden to conventional wisdom, and we should not be so if we want to solve big problems.*

For example, it is my opinion that the rules and norms governing the following activities and topics—many of which I outline in this book—were made to be thoroughly understood and then broken/discarded/tossed out the window in most cases:

- Building teams
- Establishing culture
- Contextualizing your purpose
- Selecting new team members
- Managing and enabling at scale
- Accountability

This book describes why I advocate breaking the established rules related to these topics in the cyber warfare arena so we can approach this fight in a way that gives us a competitive advantage over our hyper-focused, highly capable, and extremely nimble adversaries—and our current allies (read on for why I believe we should keep a very close eye on them in addition to our known enemies). In short, this is a book about asymmetric problem solving at scale, and although we are exploring that through the lens of cyber warfare, the principles here can be applied to any major problem in need of a solution and not just a Band-Aid.

The approach I present is informed by lessons I have learned through a lifetime of fighting, in special ops, in Brazilian jiujitsu, in business, or just through my own intuition, and demonstrates how these techniques can be applied to the most significant national security challenges we face today. It is a formula I have used with much success: an alternative, unconventional approach to actually solving problems instead of just treating symptoms. It is also about inspiration and the often-overlooked step of transforming inspiration into positive actions that lead to tangible results. Each chapter is framed by personal stories of my experiences in life, war, and business—stories that reinforce my rationale for breaking the rules. I do not mean to infer that combat experience, or a relatively impressive set of accolades, somehow endow me with more credibility on the topics covered herein. However, engaging in combat instantly provides a level of clarity that is harder to attain when risk of life, limb, or eyesight is not present.

Others have written on the topics of leadership, motivation, and discipline through the prism of special operations; to me these topics are foundational but not central. I am going to use my current mission to assist in illuminating the formula you can use regardless of your mission. Or, if you are so inclined, to help you understand how you can further the mission of creating a competitive advantage for the United States and our interests in the Fifth Domain. In the chapters that follow, I cover these topics:

- The current state of cybersecurity (or lack thereof) in America, including a sketch of the adversary and what they hope to achieve
- How to connect people to your mission, especially when they do not fully understand what it is you are doing
- The one characteristic to look for when choosing people for your elite team—and why "passion" is not it
- The true origin of your organization's brand

- The rationale for not letting your people get too comfortable
- The most effective way to hold people accountable

And much more.

This book is a call to action, both for the individuals focused directly on cybersecurity challenges and the broader society. We need to rejuvenate the fighting spirit that has made the United States a global leader. Having something you believe in so much that you wake up and fight for it every day—that is what makes up the fabric of the country I have spent my entire adult life defending. It is hard to be completely focused on something you are passionate about, something that you believe is critical, while you are vexed about that jackass driver who cut you off on the freeway this morning or worried about being late for your first meeting at 9:00 a.m. I see an America so easily exploited and distracted by our divisions that it alarms me. There is so much more we should be thinking about, so many *real* problems we should be fixing together.

If you have purpose—whatever that purpose is—and you believe that you can have an impact, then all those things that seem overwhelming will become a lot easier to handle. Whether your purpose is helping people with post-traumatic stress disorder (PTSD), or creating a competitive advantage for your organization, or saving the whales or, as in my case, winning the war in cyberspace, this book will give you a roadmap, a direction, and practical techniques that will empower you to move forward and make a real difference.

Let's gear up and get started.

PART I

INTELLIGENCE PREPARATION OF THE BATTLEFIELD

Intelligence preparation of the battlefield (IPB) is the process for executing Sun Tzu's *Art of War* concepts:

1. Know the environment

2. Know the enemy

3. Know yourself

begin Part I with a story. This one is not about me but rather how I imagine our opponents: the pieces and the players sitting on the other side of the chess board. Not the higher-up calling the shots but rather the pawn carrying out the mundane, day-to-day operations. Maybe even a knight or a rook. The person calling the shots with this piece is only slightly more complex or sophisticated. They have financial, personal, or geopolitical interest in winning, but they generally play by the established rules of this game. Their pieces have limitations—predictable approaches, driving forces, and controls. Contrary to popular belief, they are not generally outliers. Their hierarchy of needs is the same as ours.

< >

A voice crackled over the radio as the sound of bombs exploded in the distance. It was Captain John Price, the leader of Bravo Team, keying the mic.

"Makarov, this is Price. Shepherd's in the ground. I've got your ops plan and he's got a blank check. I know you can hear me on this channel, Makarov. You and I both know you won't last a week."

Makarov keyed the mic. "And neither will you," he snarled, knowing he had lost the advantage.

Martin paused the game and chuckled. *Call of Duty* was so cool! It was his favorite way to pass the time on his lunch hour and every other chance he got. His dad gave him grief for being a thirty-four-year-old man who still played video games; he said Martin was wasting his near genius IQ on such a "dumb" activity. Martin didn't care what his old man thought. He loved the game for its suspense and for the thrill of the hunt, and he enjoyed the temporary escape from reality. But most of all he loved figuring out how to outsmart the adversary; to Martin it was like solving a puzzle or cracking a secret code. He felt a rare sense of power and control when he played the game. That he was exceptionally good at it only added to its appeal. The fact that his opponent, "Price," was a twelve-year-old kid in Florida gave the dynamic a new dimension. He was fighting a war on two fronts, and Price had no idea.

Just as he was getting ready to fire up another round of battle, he received a text:

INCOMING!

Immediately followed by another:

HURRY!

Oh, shit. "Incoming" was the shorthand he and his coworkers used for "The boss is on her way to the basement, so everybody look busy!" Martin couldn't afford to get caught being late from lunch again. He'd already been busted once this week. He pocketed his phone, pitched the remains of his half-eaten meal into the wastebasket and bolted from the breakroom toward his desk. It was a long sprint—the room was the size of a gymnasium and filled with rows upon rows of desks—unfortunately, his workstation was among the farthest away. As he wove his way through the room, he passed the desk of the one who'd sent him the warning text, his best friend Alek.

"Thanks for the heads up, man!" Martin said as he dashed by.

"No problem," Alek called after him. "See you at happy hour!"

At the end of the next row sat Sofia, an attractive coworker who was always smiling at him for some reason. As he sprinted past her, she looked up from her computer and said, "Hey, I put a little present on your desk."

"Thanks!" he panted. Finally reaching his workstation in the far back corner, he collapsed into his chair just as the boss and her entourage entered at the front of the room. Martin quickly put on his blue light glasses, shook the mouse to wake up his computer, and exhaled. He'd made it! It was then he noticed a cold energy drink on his desk. That must have been the gift Sofia was talking about. He cracked it open and took a big swig; it was just what he needed to get through the long afternoon ahead. On one of his dual monitors he opened a chat window—there were already half a dozen other windows open on each monitor, most (but not all) of them work-related—and sent Sofia a message:

Thanks, I needed that! ☺

Her reply came immediately:

You're welcome! If there's anything else you need—anything at all—you let me know. XO

Suddenly it occurred to Martin that Sofia might actually be flirting with him. He leaned back and let that entertaining thought bounce around inside his head for a moment. It was kind of fun to think about hooking up with Sofia, even if it was only in a daydream. Interacting with the opposite sex had never been easy for Martin; hell, interacting with any-one face-to-face was a challenge for him. It's not that he didn't have the desire to mix and mingle. It's just that he felt more secure and confident communicating through a screen than having to deal with the complexi-ties and pressures of direct human interaction. He thrived on the logical and the rational, and he found most people to be neither.

At any rate, Martin's imagination was running wild with Sofia when a window on one of his monitors suddenly started blinking. Clicking the mouse to expand the window, Martin received the shock of his life: the code he'd been writing for months and had inserted into the program just before lunchtime was achieving its objective. Line after line of precious data was pouring in like a tsunami.

"Georgie, come look at this," Martin whispered to his colleague at the desk beside him, unable to take his eyes off the screen.

"Yeah, give me a minute . . ."

"No, *now*," Martin replied.

Hearing the urgency in Martin's voice, Georgie leapt to his feet and rushed to Martin's workstation. He peered over Martin's shoulder at the screen, its blue light reflected in both of their eyeglasses.

"Oh, my God," Georgie said when he realized what he was seeing. "What the . . . ? Martin, you did it! You did it, mate!"

Workers at nearby desks scurried over to see what all the fuss was about. Soon Martin was surrounded by a throng of colleagues looking wide-eyed at his monitor, congratulating him, shaking his hand, clapping him on the back. His face was flush with excitement and pride, especially when he saw Sofia standing on the fringe of the group beaming at him. Just as she started to walk toward him, the boss elbowed her way through the crowd.

"What is this commotion?" she asked.

"Martin's in, ma'am!" Georgie said, pointing to Martin's monitor.

As the boss watched the data streaming in, she nodded her approval, a wide smile spreading across her characteristically stern face.

"Well done, Martin," she said, shaking his hand. "Keep a close eye on this, and report your findings to us on a daily basis."

For the next several months, Martin did just that. He collected the incoming data from the system he had accessed, moving laterally within it, watching the activity there, making reports to his superiors. He was smart to have targeted this particular system, as it had long been neglected by its architects; its security controls were outdated, and it had not been properly maintained, making it relatively easy for him to enter and move around undetected for almost a year. Over time, one open door led to another, and he was able to identify the connection points within the target systems: how multiple subcontractors were linked to military bases, the location of undersea cable network endpoints, power facilities, and more. It was exciting for Martin. He felt like he was a stealth fighter in his favorite video game.

Martin wasn't privy to what his managers were going to do with the backdoors he had opened. He suspected they were preparing to run an exploit and bring down the system at some point. If their plans did include a cyber-physical attack, he knew it could destroy critical infrastructure that would be difficult for the United States to replace at scale. Truth be told, Martin didn't think about that too much. To him the United States was a random concept far removed from his day-to-day reality on the other side of the world; besides, the ultimate objective of his work was beyond his control anyway. He had been assigned by his government to do a job, and that was to connect the dots—to find entry points into critical U.S. computer systems or networks and "walk" through them without being detected. Nothing more, nothing less.

< >

Sound familiar? Our antagonist, Martin, sounds like a lot of IT people here in the United States. Nothing particularly nefarious about him. No long beard tied to a religion many of us don't understand, no explosives strapped to his chest. Just a puzzle to solve. It is hard to "other" a guy like Martin, but it is definitely possible to beat him. Our preteen first-person shooter did—because he spent more time focused on the game and did better intelligence preparation of the battlefield.

CHAPTER 1

KNOW THE
ENVIRONMENT

*The battlefield is a scene of constant chaos. The winner will be
the one who controls that chaos, both his own and his enemy's.*

—Attributed to **Napoleon Bonaparte**

I t was the spring of 2009, and I was asleep on the ground somewhere
in the mountains, lying on a ledge underneath the poncho I'd tied
between two trees to protect me from the snow that had fallen overnight. The previous day's twenty-mile trek up and down the mountainside
carrying my sixty-plus pound rucksack had really taken it out of me. It
had been a long and grueling day of hiking, running, and crawling my
way through the rugged terrain en route to this campsite, where I had
essentially passed out from exhaustion. I'd gotten only a couple hours of
sleep when I felt a sudden jolt. Someone had kicked my makeshift tent.

Groaning, I rolled over and sat up to see a fellow candidate jogging
away from me in the breaking dawn toward one of the trucks that was
pulling up the road to pick us up for the day's activities. The other men

in the group were already there, ready to go. I reached for the alarm clock I'd set beside my head a few hours earlier only to find it dead, water-logged by melting snow. *Dammit!* The admonition "Never be late, light, or out of uniform" echoed in my skull. If you were ever late, packed too light, or out of uniform during this selection process, you were gone. In other words, if I wasn't on one of those trucks in two minutes with all my gear, my dream of being chosen as an operator would be over. One other candidate's tent remained up. The guy who had seen the gray area in the saying "Selection is an individual event" had kicked that candidate before me, but he decided he couldn't get ready in time. No way in hell I was going to let that happen to me, not on this, the second-to-last day of the selection phase. Not after I'd already put in four years and multiple combat tours with these men—my squadron—who happened to be up on the rotation to help run this particular selection event. Not after I'd practically killed myself over the previous few months to make it to this point. We'd started with hundreds of candidates, and we were now down to a few dozen. I intended to be one of the last men standing. Or at least be able to hold my head up when I walked into the squadron bay for the next mission.

I rushed to pull on my boots—didn't even bother to tie them—scrambled to my feet, shoved my camping gear into the rucksack, and sprinted for the closest truck, leaping inside just as it pulled away. This incident reminded me of one of the most significant missions I'd ever been on with this squadron that was running our selection. It had happened three years prior and was chronicled in General (ret.) Stanley McChrystal's book *Team of Teams*. We had been tracking a particular high-value target (HVT) for quite some time, and he had continued to slip through the fingers of the Joint Special Operations Task Force (JSOTF) time after time. We eventually got to his spiritual advisor, and after tracking him for over three weeks, we finally got the pattern-of-life indicator[1] that he would be meeting with our guy—in the middle of the day. We'd received the page alert while we were all sleeping. I'd grabbed my gear, run to the helicopter, jumped in, and sat in the open door. As we were taking off over the crossed swords monument outside the U.S. Embassy in Baghdad, I had to lean out—anchored only by a strap attached to my belt—to tie my boots.

We hit a bump and I returned, mentally, from my reverie, to find myself back in the mountains. Sitting across from me in the back of the truck was Matt, the guy who'd kicked me awake. I looked up, made eye contact with him for a brief moment, and thanked him. Operator selection is an individual event, and we were not expected to help each other, yet for some reason this guy had helped me. If not for his well-placed and altruistic kick, I would have been disqualified and sent home with my tail between my legs. We did not really know one another, but he was one of the few who did not think I was a plant given that I was the only active unit member going through selection. (A "plant," as you might surmise, is an individual inserted into the exercise to observe the candidates outside of the physical events—their attitudes and engagements and their overall demeanor and interactions.) He later explained that he did not think a plant would make it look as hard as I did. I felt an immense rush of gratitude for Matt, but that warm feeling was quickly replaced by the stark realization that I had yet another day of hell ahead of me.

As we rumbled along this unknown road toward God knows where, I thought about what I'd been through so far on this journey to becoming

---

1   It may be useful to explain this term. Basically, people have a tendency to repeat patterns. They visit their grandmother at the nursing home every Saturday, take the same path to church on Sunday, and get coffee from their favorite shop before picking up kids from school. There is a routine (pattern), and there are patterns to routine deviation that indicate that particular day won't be like the previous day. For example, if you see the kids go to the bus stop, you can anticipate that the day will include the coffee shop and pick up on Wednesday for jiujitsu class. You can also anticipate that it will not happen if the kids do not go to the bus stop. That change is a pattern-of-life indicator that enables prediction of future action.

an operator. There were two phases to the process: the instruction phase and the selection phase. During the instruction phase, which lasted a little over a week, we lived in barracks and attended training in which concepts and activities were broken down to their most basic forms so that, no matter your background or branch, you would be given all the information and skills you needed for the selection phase, through which you demonstrated what you knew and proved that you had the right stuff. What happens during this process is a highly guarded secret. We were never told what to expect, how it would work, or what the standards would be.

For me, one of the most memorable omissions had been the fact that we would not be provided with any chairs during the instruction phase. I arrived in the barracks to find nowhere to sit. No couches, no seating of any kind (we weren't allowed to sit on our beds). The guys I had been doing missions with for the previous four years were the same ones running the instruction and selection processes, yet none of them had bothered to mention this important piece of information to me. I remember sitting on the floor in the barracks that first day, my back against the wall, totally pissed off that not one of my buddies had told me to bring a chair. Meanwhile, every guy who had been there before and had not quite made the grade, and who thus had come home unsuccessful, knew that tidbit of info. That one simple thing—the lack of a comfortable place to sit—is one of the many reasons why most people do not make it through selection and those who do usually do not make it on the first try. I have learned that something as seemingly inconsequential as a small comfort, a slim advantage, or a missed detail can be the difference between success and failure. If you want to quit, you will find an excuse. It is a law of human nature.

I had made it through that unwelcome surprise and many more that I cannot disclose, and now here I was in the final hours of this mountaineering and advanced navigation ordeal about to discover what final challenges our cadre—my mates—had in store for us. After a short ride, the trucks pulled over, and we were set loose to find our way to the next of our series of rendezvous points (RV). Other than the heavy gray mist that blanketed the mountain and reduced visibility to practically zero, it was not so bad. At the end of the day, they picked us up, but this time they did not take us to a campsite like they usually did. They took us instead to a spot on the side of a road and dumped us out with our rucksacks to begin the culminating event affectionately known as "The Long Walk," the last physical activity we had to complete in the selection process. They gave each of us a new color and number (the way we would be identified as we approached each new RV), and one by one we were released to begin our trek, which consisted of an advanced land navigation for a ludicrous distance through extremely treacherous terrain—actual distance, as I would learn, may vary. I was turned loose at 1:40 a.m. After having spent the past month hiking and climbing up and down mountains with a sixty-plus pound rucksack (depending on how wet it was, whether it was frozen, and how much water I still had in it), I was already nearing exhaustion. Still, I started my walk without a single thought of failure.

On my way to my first RV, I had to walk through a marsh, completely soaking me from the waist down. I made it through that and commenced hiking up the mountain. Within an hour my pants had frozen and both CamelBaks containing my water had frozen as well. The only potable fluid I had were some six-hour energy drinks. So, as I walked along, I drank seven of those (a tactic I do not recommend), which would be the only hydration I would have for thirteen hours until the next day when the sun came out and the water in the CamelBak drink tubes thawed. As I came down off one slope approaching an RV, I glanced to my left and saw what looked like a giant stuffed bunny rabbit and a bear sitting around a campfire. I had just enough lucidity left to realize that I was hallucinating.

I stumbled into the RV and told them what my designation was—a color and number that had evolved to something more comical—and they gave me the coordinates to find my next RV. No other words were spoken between us. While this was taking place, I heard another candidate coming into the RV behind me. We tried never to be too close to one another to avoid any suspicion that we were helping each other or asking for help, so I ducked over to the other side of the truck that was parked there and started mapping my coordinates. Once I was sure the other guy was gone, I started on my way.

However, because I started out from that side of the truck, I did not see that there was a slight (maybe one degree) alteration to the trail, so I went to the left instead of the right. Thanks to this tiny wrong turn, I ended up getting stuck in mountain laurel, a thick spiderweb of intertwining branches. Soon I was so deep into the undergrowth that I was not able to walk out. I had to take off my rucksack and crawl on my hands and knees, dragging myself, and my rucksack, through this thicket to the other side of the mountain. I continued to hallucinate, taking tiny sips of water from my CamelBak as it thawed. Eventually, I saw an opening in front of me, a creek that led down to an active waterfall.

During the instruction phase, our trainers had taught us that we were there to participate in a selection process; we were not there to die. Thus, we were told that if we ever found ourselves in moving water, we should take the buckle off our waistband and chest band and hold the quick release so that we could drop our rucksack if we got swept under. You would not make it through selection if that happened, but at least you would not drown.

Having hiked in horrible conditions for anywhere from twelve to twenty-five miles every day for a month, while consuming insufficient water for thirteen hours, I was not exactly in my right mind. Much as I may have remembered my training, I was definitely not making the most rational decisions. I started climbing down that ninety-foot waterfall (my semi-lucid estimate of the height, anyway). I unbuckled the bands and held the quick release as I did so, my rucksack swinging beneath me as I descended. If I would have slipped—which was entirely possible given the fact that there was snow and ice everywhere—I would have been dashed against the rocks on the way down and plunged into frigid water at the bottom. Grasping at the rocks with one hand and holding the quick release with the other, I switched from hand to hand as I inched my way down the waterfall. Looking back on this now, I consider it a miracle that I made it.

Once at the bottom, I paused to get my bearings. On one side of me was a raging river caused by snow melt and on the other, a cliff covered in mountain laurel. I tried to climb up the cliff, but it was too steep. I was stumbling along the riverbank when I heard traffic on the radio in my rucksack. It was a helicopter pilot talking about searching for me. We had each been given a radio to use in case of emergency; I had put mine inside an ammo can, wrapped that can in a poncho liner, and buried it deep in my rucksack to protect it. But here is the thing—my radio was not turned on. The voice I was hearing was not real. I was hallucinating again. I shook myself out of my delirium and kept walking. My goal had changed in a moment of weakness from successfully completing the final trek to avoiding having to take out the radio and ask for the help to come find me.

About a half mile downriver, I looked up the slope above me and saw someone wearing a brown skullcap walking along the ridge. The only person in the selection process who wore a cap like that was the guy who had kicked me awake more than thirty hours before. I knew that if he was up there, there must be a trail. I summoned all the strength I had and crawled up the slope through the mountain laurel on my hands and knees. Sure enough, when I reached the top, I found myself standing on a trail. Finally! By this time, the man wearing the skullcap was around 300 meters ahead of me on the footpath, and I saw that he was not the participant who had awakened me the previous day. It was just some civilian hiker who liked the trail that intersected our selection course and happened to wear a brown skullcap.

I reoriented myself and started running. An hour later I trotted into the next RV. One of the guys that I had previously deployed with was manning this particular checkpoint and as he handed me my next set of coordinates, he looked me over with an expression that said, *Man, it was a good effort, but there's no way you're going to make it.*

I plotted out my way forward and started jogging again until I ran straight into an ascent directly up the side of a mountain. I considered my options: I could take a trail and wind my way up, or I could take the mountain head on. I knew that with all the time I had lost being stuck in the brambles and picking my way down the waterfall, I was running out of time. I weighed the consideration that, at any minute, the rescue crew could come get me and tell me it was too late, the event was over. I could not let it end like that. I was going to leave everything I had out on the field.

So I climbed that mountain.

Once at the top of the ridge, I put my head down and ran for the next four hours until I reached my destination: the end of my Long Walk. I came in at an embarrassingly slow time—the last of the candidates to make it successfully. I was greeted by a very familiar face, Pat, who had just taken the reigns as the new Selection Sergeant Major. He congratulated me and asked me how I felt.

"I feel like I was beaten to death and frozen," I replied.

He directed me to sit by a campfire off in the distance. Thus, the finish line for that last part of the walk—after the four-hour run across the top of the ridge, which had felt like the longest leg of the journey—was barely a quarter mile down a tree break used for running power cables across the mountain. Only one other successful candidate remained there, having come in just ahead of me. They brought us big mugs of hot mulled wine, and he and I commenced to thawing from the inside out. Once we'd had a chance to decompress, a van arrived to pick us up. At this point, however, my legs no longer functioned. One of the cadre threw my ruck into the van and the other candidate helped me up. We were driven back to the same barracks we had occupied during the instruction phase, except now they were furnished with comfortable sofas and a television. I walked in, dropped my stuff, put my feet up on the couch and passed out. When I woke up the next morning my ankles were swollen as big as my thighs.

I felt awful, but I still had one last hoop to jump through before I could claim my prize: an intense interview with the selection board. I was summoned for this meeting first thing in the morning after coming in from the mountains. When I walked into the room (or, more accurately, lurched into the room) I found myself surrounded by familiar faces. Pat, of course, was there, as was my former squadron commander and other senior leaders whom I knew well. They had been on missions with me; I had worked for them. I had wins and losses in their eyes. This interview was intended to be a solemn occasion, and their stoic demeanor reflected that. They asked me if I had received any advance information about the selection process.

"No, and frankly I'm pissed off about it," I replied.

"Why is that?" one of them asked.

"Someone could have at least told me to bring a chair."

I could see Pat curl up in a ball trying to suppress his laughter, which gave me a moment's relief during the interrogation. At the end, I was asked to step outside and await the verdict. After a few minutes Pat came out, stood before me, and extended his hand.

"Welcome to the fraternity, Jeff," he said.

I did not register much of what Pat said after that, but it was somewhere along the lines of "This selection process now belongs to you. It's your job to protect it and bring the right people into it so we can continue to build on the mission that we started decades ago."

I will never forget the way those words made me feel. It was the proudest moment of my life.

Operator selection was the hardest thing I've ever gone through, but I actually made it harder on myself than it had to be. If I had anticipated the likelihood of melting snow and put my alarm clock on the other side of my head that night, if I had brought a chair, if I had put those CamelBaks closer to my body so they would not have frozen, and if I had been more precise and not erroneously deviated slightly to the left on that last trail, the battle would have been a more efficient and less painful experience for me.

And that is why I tell you this story. If you are going to climb a mountain, fight a battle, solve a problem, or face adversaries of any kind, the more you know about the terrain you are operating on, and the more anticipatory you are about the conditions you may encounter, the better off you are. Knowing the environment is your starting point—then you build outward and upward from there.

THE NEWS FROM THE FRONT

On the very morning in December 2020 that I sat down to start writing this book, news broke that hackers had gained access to FireEye—one of the world's largest computer security firms—and stolen the tools the company used to detect and plug cybersecurity gaps for their clients, including the Department of Homeland Security and U.S. intelligence agencies. Speculation was that the hackers were operating on behalf of a foreign government, most likely Russia. According to the Cyber Security Forum Initiative (CSFI), the stolen FireEye tools could be used in ransomware attacks, most notably against the health-care sector that was fully immersed in the process of responding to the COVID-19 pandemic at the time of the breach. FireEye CEO Kevin Mandia said that he had never seen an attack like this in his twenty-five years working in cybersecurity.

"We are witnessing an attack by a nation with top-tier offensive capabilities," Mandia wrote. "The attackers . . . are highly trained in operational security and executed with discipline and focus. They operated clandestinely, using methods that counter security tools and forensic examination. They used a novel combination of techniques not witnessed by us or our partners in the past."[2]

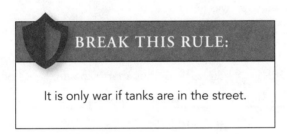

BREAK THIS RULE:

It is only war if tanks are in the street.

The FireEye attack was so serious that the FBI stepped in to investigate. The U.S. House of Representatives' Select Committee on Intelligence summoned FireEye executives for testimony about the potential exposure to our critical infrastructure and the cybersecurity community's response to the breach. For those of us who work in cybersecurity, it was a sobering moment to realize that one of our industry's most highly regarded firms had been owned—beaten at its own game—"pwned," as they say in video game parlance.

---

2   Kevin Mandia, "FireEye Shares Details of Recent Cyber Attack, Actions to Protect Community," *FireEye Stories Blog*, December 8, 2020, https://www.fireeye.com/blog/products-and-services/2020/12/fireeye-shares-details-of-recent-cyber-attack-actions-to-protect-community.html.

Unfortunately, it turned out that the FireEye breach was only the tip of the iceberg. Just four days later, another report indicated that hackers had gained access to U.S. Treasury and Commerce Department email systems (and perhaps even more). That same week yet another breach was reported, this time at the U.S. Department of Energy, which is responsible for managing our nation's nuclear weapons. Again, the speculation was that the hackers were most likely Russian operatives that had been covertly embedded in the systems for months. This was front page news all around the world, with the president of Microsoft, Brad Smith, calling it "a moment of reckoning" with "the need for a strong and global cybersecurity response."[3]

On the morning the breach of the Energy Department was announced, I received a phone call from a friend not involved in cybersecurity asking for my take on what was going on.

"Why is all this stuff happening now?" she asked. "Is it really as scary as it sounds?"

"In a word, yes," I replied. "Bombs aren't exploding, and people aren't dying . . . yet. But make no mistake, this is war."

I went on to explain that FireEye's breach investigation revealed that the hackers had gained access to the aforementioned agencies through a SolarWinds back door (SolarWinds is a cyber risk firm with software that helps companies and other entities stay compliant and manage their programs). Accessing that back door gave the hackers entry into the Treasury, Commerce, and Energy departments, and potential entry into any of the approximately 33,000 private governmental support entities that use SolarWinds technology. Of those 33,000 entities, approximately 18,000 had downloaded the tainted software version. Once inside, there were multiple things the hackers could do. They could sit there and collect

3   Brad Smith, "A Moment of Reckoning: The Need for a Strong and Global Cybersecurity Response," *Microsoft on the Issues*, December 17, 2020, https://blogs.microsoft.com/on-the-issues/2020/12/17/cyberattacks-cybersecurity-solarwinds-fireeye/.

intelligence, extract or compromise the integrity of data, or launch payloads to "blow up" the network.

"Imagine if hackers got into your retirement fund and moved the decimal point of everybody's balance by two digits," I explained to my friend. "You'd go from having a hundred thousand dollars to a thousand dollars in your account in a matter of seconds. Or they could block availability, take the whole network down. Now imagine if they got access to our industrial control systems that control the energy grid, dams, water treatment facilities, and so on. Imagine if they gained control over our media, or got access to our nuclear power generation, emergency response communications systems, health-care records, or weapon system designs, or got ahold of maps of our critical infrastructure. That is happening.

"And once they get inside, it's like having spies everywhere," I continued. "If our government determines that the group responsible for these latest attacks is using certain assault tactics or has specific nefarious goals in mind, they may end up being designated an APT, or advanced persistent threat—in other words, an enemy unit, just as if they were our combatants in a physical war. So, yes, this is a scary and potentially life-threatening scenario."

"But with all our technical capabilities and all the bright minds in this country, how come we haven't been able to protect ourselves from these sorts of attacks?" she asked.

"That's an excellent question with multiple right answers," I said, "and the first has to do with the immense scale of the battlefield itself."

THE EXPANDING ATTACK SURFACE

It is probably hard (if not impossible) for younger Americans to imagine what life was like before the internet became standard issue in virtually every home, school, business, and coffee shop in the United States. But kids, I assure you that there really was a time when only a handful of linked computers existed in the entire world. Beginning in 1969, the United States launched the precursor to the internet—the Advanced Research Projects Agency Network (ARPANET)—the primary function of which was to link computers at Department of Defense (DoD) research organizations via telephone lines. Back then, there was one computer in New Mexico and three in southern California, and the only way you could get into the DoD network, for good or for ill, was through those four points. Naturally, the DoD was concerned about the security of even that small network and took steps to protect it from threats, which was not that difficult to do. ARPANET was, after all, a tiny and well-contained battlefield—a very small *attack surface*. Briefly defined, the attack surface in cyber warfare is the sum of every potential point of entry into an entity's online data or operations system.

Since the advent of ARPANET in the late 1960s, the size of the attack surface around every aspect of our lives has exploded. Virtually all the critical data generated by individuals, the military, government agencies, businesses, public utilities, and beyond is now stored in a global network of data centers that are all connected, a network otherwise known as "the cloud." People like you and me tap into this network every day when we log on to our favorite websites or any of the fifty different applications on our mobile phones, and many of those websites and apps connect to one or more of the critical infrastructure sectors I mentioned earlier (such as telecom, health care, financial services, and so on). Now the attack surface—meaning every point that somebody in cyberspace could enter and start having a negative impact on our way of life—has become enormous.

For an overview of how pervasive the threat is in our lives, check out these statistics about the scale of our current attack surface:

- In 2019, nearly 87 percent of U.S. households were linked to the internet.[4]

- There were almost 4.66 billion internet users worldwide as of January 2021.[5]

- As of 2020 there were 274 million smart phone users in the United States alone. That number is projected to reach 311 million by 2025.[6]

- In 2021, about 50 percent of all corporate data worldwide was stored in the cloud, and that percentage is expected to increase with each passing year.[7]

- In 2020, more than half (54 percent) of all U.S. government data was stored in the cloud, with a significant portion of it deemed "sensitive."[8]

- In 2020, there were 1,001 data breaches in the United States, with almost 156 million sensitive records exposed.[9]

- Nearly 100 million new malware threats are released every day.[10]

4   Joseph Johnson, "Percentage of Households with Internet Use in the United States from 1997 to 2019," *Statista*, January 27, 2021, https://www.statista.com/statistics/189349/us-households-home-internet-connection-subscription/.

5   Joseph Johnson, "Global Digital Population as of January 2021," *Statista*, September 10, 2021, https://www.statista.com/statistics/617136/digital-population-worldwide/.

6   S. O'Dea, "Number of Smart Phone Users in the United States from 2018 to 2025," *Statista*, March 19, 2021, https://www.statista.com/statistics/201182/forecast-of-smartphone-users-in-the-us/.

7   Kimberly Mlitz, "Share of Corporate Data Stored in the Cloud in Organizations Worldwide from 2015 to 2021," *Statista*, July 31, 2021, https://www.statista.com/statistics/1062879/worldwide-cloud-storage-of-corporate-data/.

8   Mariam Baksh, "Survey: Most Federal Officials Expect Cloud Service Providers to Secure Their Data," *Nextgov*, April 21, 2020, https://www.nextgov.com/it-modernization/2020/04/survey-most-federal-officials-expect-cloud-service-providers-secure-their-data/164780/.

9   Joseph Johnson, "Annual Number of Data Breaches and Exposed Records in the United States from 2005 to 2020," *Statista*, March 3, 2021, https://www.statista.com/statistics/273550/data-breaches-recorded-in-the-united-states-by-number-of-breaches-and-records-exposed/.

10   Virginia Harrison and Jose Pagliery, "Nearly 1 Million New Malware Threats Released Every Day," *CNN Business*, April 14, 2015, https://money.cnn.com/2015/04/14/technology/security/cyber-attack-hacks-security.

- One internet service provider reports 80 billion malicious scans a day.[11]
- There are 4,000 ransomware attacks every day.[12]
- In most cases an attacker is inside the network for 280 days before they are found and contained.[13]

Let's use the energy grid in my home state of Florida to illustrate the attack surface. When Florida Power and Light (FPL) was formed in the 1920s, our power was not connected to the internet, thus the attack surface on our energy delivery system was relatively small. But as soon as FPL achieved internet capability, its attack surface expanded exponentially. It expanded even more when, a few years ago, FPL published an app to enable customers to monitor their home's energy usage and pay their bills online. At the critical moment when I and thousands of other FPL customers downloaded that app, we became part of FPL's attack surface, and our power grid became exponentially more vulnerable.

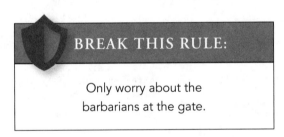

BREAK THIS RULE:

Only worry about the
barbarians at the gate.

I do not mean to single out FPL here. You could substitute any entity in this scenario, from a hospital to a bank to the DMV to the Pentagon. Recall

---

11   Jack Foster, "21 Terrifying Cyber Crime Statistics," VPN Geeks, March 17, 2021, https://www.vpngeeks.com/cyber-crime-statistics.

12   Central Intelligence Agency, "How to Protect Your Networks from Ransomware," accessed January 6, 2022, https://www.justice.gov/criminal-ccips/file/872771/download.

13   IBM, "Cost of a Data Breach Report, 2020," accessed January 13, 2021, https://www.ibm.com/security/data-breach.

the incident in Nashville on Christmas Day 2020 when one man blew up a recreational vehicle in front of an AT&T building and singlehandedly took down E-911, cell phones, and internet in the greater Nashville area for an extended period of time. My point is that the cybersecurity terrain has gotten a lot more complex, and all things critical to our way of life—like power, water, sewage, communication, health care, food distribution, transportation, and even national security mechanisms—can be interrupted purely through cyberspace. Or these entities may be identified and targeted through cyber applications and then subjected to a cyber-physical attack like the one in Nashville. Whereas previously our political adversaries, like the Russians and the Chinese, would have had to parachute in to take over a power plant, now it can be done by some smart sixteen-year-old sitting in his parents' basement in Milwaukee, Almaty, Kyiv, or Wuhan.

INTERNAL AND EXTERNAL ATTACK SURFACES

There are two tiers to an attack surface: *internal* and *external*. The *internal* attack surface consists of all the people who have authorized access to data and operations. For example, in my company, my team and I are part of the internal attack surface. We have *cover for status*, meaning we have a legitimate reason for being there, but any of us could wreak havoc if we were so inclined. According to the National Association of Corporate Directors and the Internet Security Alliance, there are five types of internal threats:[14]

- *Careless workers:* Employees or partners who nonmaliciously misappropriate resources, break acceptable use policies,

---

14   Larry Clinton, Josh Higgins, and Friso van der Oord, "Cyber-Risk Oversight, 2020," 2020, https://www.casede.org/index.php/biblioteca-casede-2-0/seguridad/ciberseguridad/537 -cyber-risk-oversight-2020/file.

mishandle data, install unauthorized applications, or use
unapproved workarounds

- *Inside agents:* Insiders recruited, solicited, or bribed by external parties to exfiltrate data

- *Disgruntled employees:* Current or former employees who intentionally destroy or steal data, or take other cyber actions to harm the employer

- *Malicious insiders:* Actors with access to corporate assets who use existing privileges to access information for personal gain

- *Feckless third parties:* Business partners who compromise security through negligence, misuse, or malicious access to, or use of, an asset.

Think back to the FireEye breach I referenced earlier. If that had been caused by a FireEye employee plugging a USB drive into a company computer and downloading FireEye's secret hacking and exploitation tools, it would have been a case of an inside agent exploiting the internal attack surface. Another example of an internal attack threat is the notorious case in 2018 in which an employee of SunTrust bank stole the bank's contact lists, compromising the sensitive data of 1.5 million clients. Other notorious perpetrators are people like Edward Snowden and Chelsea Manning.

Alternatively, the *external* attack surface consists of everybody from the outside who may want to gain unauthorized access to an entity's data and operations. Had the FireEye breach been caused by outside actors who got in through, let's say, an email phishing attack that downloaded malware enabling them to exfiltrate data from FireEye's network, that would be an example of the exploitation of the external attack surface. At the time of this writing, that is what we think happened to FireEye in late 2020.

TECHNOLOGY NOISE

Whether we are talking about a single company or an entire nation, a broad attack surface (often containing both internal and external surfaces) means that there are many technologies activated within it and even more technologies attempting to secure it. It is not unusual for an enterprise to partner with dozens of different security vendors who have built various technologies to solve specific problems, like proof of identity and access management, for example. At first glance this might look like a sensible approach. If there is a potential hole in your organization, why not partner with an expert who has built the tech to plug it? The problem is that these technologies are rarely properly implemented on their own and almost never properly integrated with each other to create a cohesive, impermeable security mesh. It is like building a safe door to your house but leaving a seam open along a wall somewhere.

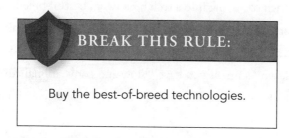

BREAK THIS RULE:

Buy the best-of-breed technologies.

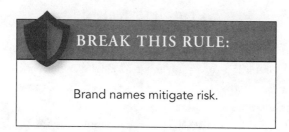

BREAK THIS RULE:

Brand names mitigate risk.

Imagine buying an ADT security system, a Ring doorbell, static cameras, and motion-sensing lights to protect your house. These may be the best-of-breed for their individual capabilities, but if they are challenging or impossible to integrate and operate, their ability to achieve the objective of enhanced security is diminished or even lost. Once you add in all the batteries going out at different times, having to aim every one of the cameras and sensor lights in precisely the right directions to ensure seamless coverage, conscientiously locking all the doors and closing all the windows—and remembering to turn the system on every day—you are setting yourself up to be exploited despite your best-laid plans. Wi-Fi connection or Bluetooth may protect you from the random thug, but it leaves you vulnerable to the cat burglar with some enhanced tech skills.

This is what I refer to as *technology noise*. Companies and individuals cannot possibly stay up with the most recent security technology. There is just too much of it and the development pace is frantic. And there's no incentive for the firms offering solutions to particular problems to integrate with other pieces of tech. Most of the time, organizations adopt the conventional approach of buying into a tech because it's best-of-breed, not because it works seamlessly with the other tools they already have in place to meet their specific needs. By now you know what I think of the conventional approach. It works fine if you have a slow and conventional adversary, but for today's highly sophisticated threats a conventional defense is not enough.

DEFINITION

Technology noise is the barrage of stimuli emanating largely from vendors intended to create fear and inspire confidence, only to result in being tuned out by both business and residential consumers. Technology noise, among other things, consists of the emails, the ad pop-ups, the flashing fluorescent lights of trade shows, and the reports published by numerous trade publications that endlessly segment technologies so the companies can buy their way into a "leader," "innovator," or "best-in-show" status.

We in the industry are not helping matters. We are just building more tools and trying to unseat other vendors. Every time there is news of a breach somewhere, all the competitors of the compromised cybersecurity firm swoop in to try to snag all their accounts. The process of taking off one vendor's technology and adding another's in and of itself creates a massive and recurring number of security gaps. The attack surface resembles a chicken-wire canoe when you are in the middle of a tech transition like that.

The worst part is that we Americans are all in that leaky canoe together, and we are in danger of sinking if we don't rally to take control of this vast battlefield and work collectively to outmaneuver our adversaries. But before we can beat them, we have to identify the "enemy" and, just as importantly, *seek to understand them.*

CHAPTER 2

KNOW THE ENEMY

*Pay attention to your enemies, for they
are the first to discover your mistakes.*

—**Antisthenes,** quoted in Diogenes Laertius,
Lives and Opinions of the Eminent Philosophers

I can understand the emotional reaction most of us would have when we hear about a suicide bombing, the detonation of a dirty bomb in a major metropolitan area, or the beheading of a hostage. We are shocked and appalled, probably even sickened by the gory details. We cannot understand what would possess a fellow human being to kill and maim innocent men, women, and children, especially in such horrific ways. There is only one explanation that makes sense to us: the perpetrators of these deeds are crazy and evil to their core.

That is the wrong assumption to make if your goal is to prevent future attacks on the ground and in cyberspace.

BREAK THIS RULE:

Only crazy, malicious people
hurt others through tech.

Listen up, because this is important: *the key to success in special operations and asymmetric warfare is to be able to put yourself in the position of your adversaries without demonizing them.* You must be able to see the situation through their eyes without your emotions clouding your view, because looking at it from their perspective will enable you to better predict, prepare, respond, and defeat them.

OUR OPPONENTS HAVE
TWO ADVANTAGES OVER US:

1. Most of us don't realize we are at war.
2. We dismiss them as crazy, evil, and/or short sighted.

This ability to empathize with the enemy is one of the main differences between conventional warfare and special operations. In a conventional war you want your troops and the folks back home to view the adversary as deranged and evil because that is the mindset that is going to motivate them to fight (or support the fight). Factionalism—extracting old grudges and fostering a good-versus-evil mentality—is a common tool of those seeking to achieve control and build momentum for a cause.

The act of "othering" is so prolific that you even see it in the pop-up targets on military rifle ranges. Multiple studies have shown that even when troops are compelled to fire their weapons in combat, most will intentionally miss. This is the military adaptation of the Pareto Principle or the 80/20 rule: out of every 100 soldiers, eighty are just targets, nineteen are going to fight and one is the leader who will bring them home. If most people, by their nature, will intentionally miss, then you have to train them such that if they are ever faced with a specific enemy, they are predisposed to actually hit the target. Get the troops normalized to shooting at the adversary they must expect. Teach them: *these are the bad guys, and you have to shoot them because they are evil.* If you are shooting just another human being, it is murder. If you are shooting someone who is evil, it is acceptable—admirable, even.

"Othering" is so conventional that you also see it in religious discussions, in the vitriol of the media, and most definitely in our binary political structure. It is conventional, first and foremost, because it is effective. By fashioning a compelling and demonic image of the other and rallying the troops against that image, the protagonist leaders have successfully oversimplified complex issues and can count on a predictable and manageable emotional response from their followers, a response that triggers a refusal among the followers to consider alternatives or to engage in dialogue. This makes the jobs of the powers-that-be easier, but it also makes it easier for our adversaries to manipulate and exploit us because this dumbed-down viewpoint complicates our battle preparation, response, and recovery.

For those of us charged with defeating adversaries in the Fifth Domain, embracing conventional factionalism serves no purpose. If the enemy is just crazy or evil then any attempt to understand their tactics, motivation, and other considerations is not only impossible—it might actually be dangerous. That is why, in asymmetric warfare and special operations, we are taught that you do not win by assuming the other side is crazy or evil because then you cannot put yourself in their shoes. You cannot predict the "art of the possible," which is a common term in the special ops community I grew up in. It means throwing out conventional wisdom, thinking outside the box and exploring all the things you *could* do, not just what you are supposed to do. It means being able to see the situation from the adversary's perspective. This is where our fictional friend Martin (a.k.a. Makarov) from the opening of Part I comes into play. He is not a wholly unlikable guy. Faces the same challenges many of us face—an overbearing boss, loneliness, a twelve-year-old punk from Florida who seems to have memorized the weapons storage map in *Call of Duty*, and a girl in the office he wants to impress.

DEFINITION

The art of the possible is a euphemism for a mindset that is not constrained by traditional wisdom. It's not about doing what is "right" or "best," but what you can actually get done. It's about exploring the alternative avenues you *could* take to achieve your desired outcome. It's about opening your mind—individually and collectively—such that you are not constrained by barriers and limits.

Up to now, the American people have not been taught to imagine the world from the adversary's point of view and to explore the art of the possible. In my opinion, this is why we have been getting pwned, infiltrated, and manipulated by bad actors who are playing short-term, mid-term, and long-term games in cyberspace. How do I know? Beyond what I read in the press and what I have personally seen, *it is what I would do if I were them.* This goes beyond the overt adversarial relationships we are all familiar with (hello Russia, China, Iran, and North Korea!). Those adversaries are concerning, obviously, but because we know them, they are usually the easiest to mobilize against and build defenses for. We watch their tape (or videos!) and know many of their plays. It is our allies and currently inconsequential actors on the world stage who can lull us to sleep and become adversaries when we least expect it. Those are the ones who keep me up at night. They should keep you up at night as well.

Let's get to know these rivals and attempt to understand them with clear eyes and open minds, for only then will we be able to think about how we would operate if we were in their shoes. Once we have that knowledge and understanding of the enemy, we can create the mechanisms to beat them.

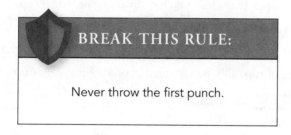

BREAK THIS RULE:

Never throw the first punch.

PROFILE OF A CYBERSPACE WARRIOR

Before we examine this profile, I want to reiterate that we should not assume that all nation state-labeled cyberattacks are coming from Russia, China, North Korea, and Iran. They could also come from our allies and potential future adversaries. The hackers could be of any nationality, color, age, creed, or political ideology. They could be former intelligence operatives who have gotten too old for that line of work yet still want to be involved. Or they could fit the following general profile of a cyberspace warrior like Martin (a.k.a. Makarov), our friend from the opening of Part I. The cyberspace warrior is most typically (but not always) male, so I use he/him/his pronouns here for simplicity's sake. Of course, there are exceptions to the generalizations presented in this profile, but I consider the following sketch to be a fair representation of one of the more prolific archetypes.

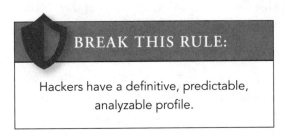

BREAK THIS RULE:

Hackers have a definitive, predictable, analyzable profile.

Our hacker character identified in the intro is probably in his thirties. He grew up watching spy movies, and video games were his refuge. He really likes things that challenge him in terms of strategy, so beating the different levels of a video game is highly motivating to him. He may have played some sports when he was in school. He has a higher-than-average IQ and would probably be classified psychologically as an introvert. He doesn't understand why his interactions with other people are not more comfortable and logical.

Despite his feelings of discomfort around others, the cyber warrior's personal life looks fairly normal by all outward appearances. He probably has a girlfriend or a wife and kids. The way he interacts with his family may be perfectly fine. Still, he doesn't believe he's normal; he feels misunderstood. He seeks refuge in the dark web and in chat rooms, where he can engage with like-minded people who feed his curiosity and challenge him in ways that others around him cannot.

As for his professional life, he may work in a company that is owned by an intelligence service or a nation state, or he may be a foreign government agent who has been strategically placed in a sleeper position within an unsuspecting consulting firm or technology company, or even a well-known organization like Boeing, Pfizer, or Deloitte. His job may be collecting information, putting malware into the code he's writing for these companies, or embedding hardware technologies into servers, switches, endpoints, and the like. Or he may have worked for a time at a U.S. defense contractor and surreptitiously built back doors into their systems, and now he works in a highly secured government facility where he breaks into his former American employer's systems using the back doors he created. He monitors what's happening there, providing his government with reports. Or he collects data and releases payloads at his government's behest. And just to be clear, his "government" could be an adversarial regime or a supposed allied nation, or he could be working for a criminal syndicate either in-country or overseas. He may be the lead software developer or engineer in a cybersecurity firm, and he is making sure a back door is getting placed in the design of everything his team is doing.

Alternatively, he could be a member of one of the threat-posing groups I outline in Chapter 1. In that case, he could be sitting in a server farm in Bulgaria (or pick another country; it is happening all over the world). In this role, he is looking for back doors to open or walk through. He is monitoring those elements that were placed deliberately by others and generating intelligence reports and then pushing those reports to people whose job is finding mechanisms to exploit the information they contain. He may have written a damaging code, and then his organization may employ a local agent (female, attractive, fun) to strike up a relationship with a married American security analyst and blackmail him into plugging a thumb drive with the code into his network to avoid having incriminating pictures sent to his wife.

Or, rather than writing code, our warrior could be involved in voice phishing, or "vishing." In this practice, he calls unsuspecting people and acts as if he is a customer service representative from the bank, telephone, or utility company to get his target to reveal sensitive data. In the park, he may be a kind stranger asking verification questions like, "What was your first dog's name?" which can be used to execute credentials in a subsequent cyberattack. Or he could be involved in sifting through trash for account numbers or other confidential information.

The bottom line: our cyber warrior hacker is focused exclusively on illuminating and attacking critical infrastructure nodes across the United States. All these things are done in combination, slowly, over long periods of time. Consequently, it requires a tremendous amount of patience.

Interestingly, it is possible that our cyber warrior fell into this line of work by getting into trouble when he was younger. He likely got arrested for hacking into a banking system or some other supposedly secure system when he was in his late teens or early twenties. Because he had demonstrated valuable computer skills, he was put into a dark room and given a series of options—none of which were very good, especially if he was in North Korea, Iran, Russia, or China. He could (a) be executed, (b) go to prison for the rest of his life, or (c) work for the government. He chose option c, at which point he was trained and repurposed as a cyber warrior for the state. It is just a different variation of a prison sentence, essentially.

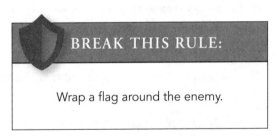

BREAK THIS RULE:

Wrap a flag around the enemy.

This young man does not have to hate you or me or America. The places he is attacking and the people he's affecting are not real to him. He is not necessarily an ideologue. The people above him are the ideologues. They are the ones who believe in the cause; they are the ones motivated by their flag (or perhaps, their faith). Our guy? Not so much. He's motivated by the challenge his work provides. For him it is just another game, another series of levels to unlock. It's about the cool tools and tech he gets to use. It's about the coworkers sitting to his left and to his right every day, people just like him. People who appreciate his skills. *People who understand him.*

These are our adversaries, the pieces on the other side of the game board. Each could be a man, woman, or nonbinary. Any race, creed, color, or age. They could execute one of these techniques, many of them, or all of them in concert. Without an appropriate response from us, their actions become disruptive, detrimental, and ultimately, debilitating.

OPERATIONAL AND INTELLIGENCE PREPARATION FOR WAR IN THE FIFTH DOMAIN

So how do we counter them appropriately? How do we set ourselves up for maximum success? For clues, think about how we gain an advantage over our opponents in a ground war. We do not just blindly deploy cavalry units and drop bombs willy-nilly. We do a lot of advance planning and positioning of assets. We analyze how the adversaries conduct their operations, how they enable their logistics, and how they communicate with one another, among many other factors. Once we identify those elements we can disrupt them, thereby weakening our opponent considerably. Patience is the name of this game, and those who are the best at it will be the winners.

In the military, we call this groundwork process *operational preparation of the environment* (OPE) and IPB. In carrying out these activities, we identify facts and assumptions about the battlefield environment and the threats involved, enabling staff planning and the development of friendly courses of action (COA).

One of the most brilliant examples of OPE and IPB in modern times occurred in the year leading up to D-Day in World War II. Well in advance of the Normandy invasion, the allies successfully controlled communication pathways and served the Nazis a dazzling array of fake intelligence designed to divert Hitler's attention away from their intended landing place on the beaches of Normandy. British intelligence officers flipped a number of Germans who acted as double agents, intentionally feeding false information to Berlin.

Among other tactics, the allies engaged in bogus radio chatter to make Hitler think that they were going to attack him in a variety of places, including Scandinavia. They even used inflatable tanks and constructed phony airplanes out of painted canvas stretched over metal frames, which they then positioned to convince the Nazis that they were lining up to launch assaults elsewhere. At the same time, they dropped people behind the lines to identify where all the guns were so those could be taken out at the beginning, in the hours prior to the main assault. All that work was done well in advance of putting soldiers on boats and ferrying them across the English Channel.

That is how the good guys won World War II. But here is the kicker: that kind of preparation happens constantly whether you're nearing a war or not. This is the same kind of activity our adversaries are engaged in against us today in cyberspace. The intelligence and operations they have performed and are continuing to perform will determine the competitive advantage they will gain over us.

Right now, cyber warriors around the world are laying the groundwork, doing OPE and IPB for any number of attacks against us. In the Fifth Domain, OPE includes activities like building a back door into a critical infrastructure system so you can take control whenever you want to, or teaching Chinese and Russian spies the latest cloud native languages with the goal of getting them hired into security companies in Silicon Valley.

Conversely, IPB is all the intelligence-related activity that supports the major power competition that's happening in cyberspace. It includes mapping out where all of the important networks are, identifying how they connect to the global information grid, and understanding who the key players are so they can be targeted for exploitation. For example, our adversaries might identify an engineer for an American power company—say, someone who is the global administrator of all the power systems on the Eastern seaboard—and then deploy one of their attractive female agents to reach out to him through Instagram pretending to be someone she's not. One thing leads to another, and the engineer and agent enter into a clandestine relationship. Next thing you know, the engineer's mistress has compromising pictures of him—pictures that can be used to exploit him, control him, and make him do nefarious things that he would never do otherwise. If you think this kind of drama only happens in spy movies, you are dead wrong. Our adversaries are focused and creative. They are smart and unscrupulous, and they are operating against us 24/7.

Now let us explore the current state of cybersecurity in America, our conventional approach to dealing with our challenges, and why we have been unable to protect ourselves so far.

CHAPTER 3

KNOW YOURSELF

If you know the enemy and know yourself,
you need not fear the results of a hundred battles.

—**Sun Tzu,** *The Art of War*

I t does not matter how badass you are; eventually you are going to run into someone who can eat your lunch. Once you understand that, and I mean *really* understand it, it frames the way you engage in fights or conflict from that day forward. You no longer fight for sport; you fight only to win. *Win or Die* becomes your mantra. The special missions unit (SMU) I was a part of has an extremely effective method for driving home this lesson: a training event called the Black-Eyed Saloon. As legend would tell, it is based on the real-world experience of a special operator somewhere in the Balkans who once had a particularly challenging day. He had gone out for a run through the city, and when he arrived back at his hotel, he was accosted by two robbers who beat the hell out of him. A bad day taught him some important lessons about himself—lessons that made him a better operator going forward.

My trip to the Black-Eyed Saloon started with a two-mile run through a complex obstacle course. The course led me, exhausted, to a building that was meant to simulate a hotel, and there I was attacked by two men who beat me until I could no longer fight back. At that point, the controller stepped in and moved me inside the building where I was attacked in a hallway and battered until I lost that fight. From there, I was sent up a staircase, where I was again outnumbered and beaten nearly senseless. In that instant, I was pushed into an elevator where, you guessed it, I was attacked and beaten yet again. Stumbling out of the elevator, bruised and bloody, I entered a room that was set up like a saloon with a bunch of operators in it. I was told to order a drink. As I hobbled over to the bar, a brief thought crossed my mind that the drink must be my reward for making it through the exercise. As soon as I reached the bar, every man in the room jumped me. I tried to escape, making it to the doorframe, which I gripped with all my strength as blows to my abdomen landed and I was ultimately ripped from the door by my feet. The air escaped my lungs with a thud as I landed on the floor, receiving some kicks before the event was completed.

Everybody who goes through the Black-Eyed Saloon training learns something different from it, but the main takeaways for most of us are (1) no matter how good a fighter you are, at some point you are going to lose; (2) even when you lose, you will survive—no scenario's going to be deadly unless it is going to be deadly; and (3) you lose a lot faster when you are tired. Knowing these things about yourself is incredibly good for your psyche. It motivates you to become a better fighter, to pick your battles more carefully, and on the rare occasion when you do have to fight, to go all in with no holds barred. For me, that motivation induced me to acquire and fine-tune an unconventional fighting style through my practice of Brazilian jiujitsu, to the point that I have become an American and pan-American champion and risen to the rank of black belt.

The Black-Eyed Saloon was some of the most valuable training I have ever received, because as special operators, we could actually end up in a situation similar to what we went through in the exercise. We had been through the hardest selection processes in the world, we had been given millions of dollars' worth of training, and we could shoot as well as or better than anybody else. It is easy to emerge from all that with a massive ego, and exercises like the Saloon have a way of humbling you. They have a way of teaching you that there is more to winning than just throwing the most punches. More than anything else, it is about grit and endurance.

Every week I see guys come into the martial arts school where I train, guys with super-jacked egos because they wrestled Division I in college and can bench press a car. These cats fully expect to excel at jiujitsu. And then they hit the mat for the first time, and their opponent, a tiny seventeen-year-old girl, ties them in knots and chokes them out. Some of them never return to the academy after that humiliation, but the others—the ones who have grit—become immediate believers and dedicate themselves completely to their training. Those are the ones you want on your team. What they lack in skills, they more than make up for in endurance and courage and determination. They are not afraid to lose because they know it means they will get better.

So, back to America's cyber warfare conundrum. We have been getting badly beaten lately; our opponents have given us more than a few black eyes in the cyberspace arena. The losses are adding up, and just like in the Black-Eyed Saloon, there are even more adversaries around the next corner. However, that does not mean we are down for the count. We can summon our grit and stand up for the next round. But before we do, we must make an honest, humble assessment of where we are right now.

COMPLIANCE AT A SNAIL'S PACE

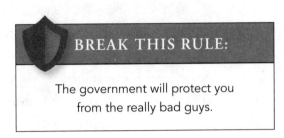

BREAK THIS RULE:

The government will protect you
from the really bad guys.

There is a lot of activity around our response to cyber warfare in the United States but, unfortunately, not many good outcomes. Federal agencies are working on this, but the problem is that most of the things that support our way of life are happening within critical infrastructure sectors. The federal agencies provide guidance and frameworks and have set up information-sharing resources like Infragard, but the problem is too big and too widespread for them to handle on their own. Over three hundred thousand companies are part of the U.S. defense industrial base, and the DoD is not monitoring those systems. Instead, they are asking those companies to protect those networks themselves. If you expand the lens beyond DoD and look at health care, financial services, energy, and so on, there is way too much for the government to protect without all those critical infrastructure sectors doing their part. Not only are our compliance standards challenging for companies to meet, but the standards themselves are also ineffective. Organizations tend to respond only when compelled by a regulatory burden, essentially not owning cybersecurity until the Securities and Exchange Commission (SEC) starts fining them for noncompliance or breach, or until there is some other financial risk. All these things affect us.

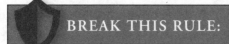

BREAK THIS RULE:

As long as you meet compliance
standards, you are safe.

Cybersecurity compliance standards significantly trail behind the broad realization of risk. They are reactive, and they are way too slow. If a company is doing their cybersecurity based purely on a compliance standard—which many are—it is because a significant portion of their industry was already owned by an attacker. Here is what happens next: Once everyone realizes that there was an attack, they elevate the issue to policy makers. The policy makers have a bunch of lobbyists come in and help write a bill, and that bill subsequently gets assigned to an executive branch agency. That executive branch agency creates a compliance framework for the organizations regulated by their agency. They establish a team to go in and do verifications to make sure the organizations are conforming to the standards. By the time they get around to running those checks, we are two or three years out from the original events, and the adversary has reinvented itself hundreds of times. In other words, by the time we have a compliance standard in place, it is too late. The adversary knows exactly which doors we are going to lock, so they build tools to go in through the window.

A LACK OF HANDS ON DECK

We currently have 3.5 million unfilled cyber roles in America,[15] and we also are making no *effectively coordinated* effort to solve the problem. Read

---

15   James Andrew Lewis and William Crumpler, "The Cyber Security Workforce Gap," Center
      for Strategic and International Studies, January 29, 2019, https://www.csis.org/analysis/cyber
      security-workforce-gap.

that sentence again. If you are not shocked by that, you should be. We are woefully outgunned. Some would argue that stat, but I can tell you that finding and retaining talent is a real challenge.

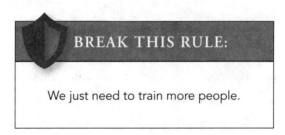

BREAK THIS RULE:

We just need to train more people.

Our industry has a massive talent gap, and the impact of that sad fact is that we have unqualified people moving into positions of leadership. When you have three and a half million (or whatever the real number is) unfilled positions, you are not going to be able to pick the brightest, most fully qualified chief information security officer (CISO). Since there is not a lot of competition for the leadership positions, we continue to have people in those jobs who cannot manifest a vision and implement a program that works. They are going to continue taking the conventional approach because that is what they are measured against.

We have leaders making technology decisions based primarily on marketing fund-fueled publications, like *Gartner Magic Quadrant* and *Forrester Wave*, highlighting best-of-breed technologies that take twelve to twenty-four months to implement. The average life expectancy of a CISO in any given company is somewhere around eighteen to twenty-four months.[16] If the organization gets owned while the risk management technology is being put in place, it cannot be the CISO's fault, right? After all, they were implementing the technology like they were supposed to. They could not have possibly achieved the outcome because

---

16   "What's the Deal with CISO Burnout?" CyberTalk.org, October 15, 2019, https://www
      .cybertalk.org/2019/10/15/whats-the-deal-with-ciso-burnout/.

of the time constraint. And if the organization gets owned after they fully implemented their plan, odds are it is not going to be discovered for 280 days (remember: that's the average amount of time an attacker is on a network before getting caught). By then, our CISO will be long gone.

The lack of ownership and expertise in our industry means that all anyone is expected to do is to move toward compliance. Compliance is not the same as maturity and is a far cry from effectiveness. Compliance means that I am doing what I'm supposed to do today, while maturity means that I'm doing what I'm supposed to do *every day*. Effectiveness, on the other hand, means that what I am doing every day actually works. Most organizations never get to maturity, let alone effectiveness.

We discuss compliance, maturity, and effectiveness again in Chapter 7. For now, know that we have at best a compliance-based culture within our critical infrastructure sectors. At worst, very little attention is paid to actual security and privacy with no real sense of all the potential threats that could infect our systems and degrade our way of life. The SEC is doing more enforcement and shifting responsibility for cybersecurity up to the board level, but most boards do not have the technical competency or the experience to be able to make good decisions. Even if they wanted to keep pace, the technology is changing so rapidly, making it incredibly difficult to keep up.

This is the current state of our cyber warfare readiness (or lack thereof), and this is why we must reject it immediately.

WHO ARE YOU, REALLY?

The other night at jiujitsu practice, I had an interesting conversation with another black belt. We were talking about how each of us developed our unique fighting styles, and we decided that our success began with our capacity to know ourselves intimately, inside and out. Sadly, most people go through their lives not really knowing who they are, thereby limiting their ability to reach their full potential.

In my case, my jiujitsu style is very much like my style in business, which bleeds over into every other aspect of my life. What it appears I am doing is typically not what I am doing. I use all the tools at my disposal in nontraditional ways. I am not satisfied with winning a match on points. I am determined to finish the fight.

That is the mentality I grew up with in special operations. The motto of the team I was on is "Oppressors beware." Our guiding principles are those of close-quarters battle (CQB): "speed, surprise, and violence of action." That is counter to the way most jiujitsu is done. Traditional jiujitsu is about learning established sequences, doing a lot of drilling. Once you learn all the standard moves (around the time you are a purple belt), you start to develop your own personal style. In other words, after you have learned sound technique to the point that it has become second nature, you are free to spread your wings. That is when the art and the magic start to happen. That is when your uniquely personal power is actualized.

In the military we learn the standard approaches, the conventional wisdom, the time-tested structures—all of that. They are drilled into us from sunup to sundown every day for years. However, when we are chosen to join special ops, we are free to reject those old structures and standards and let our own style emerge, all while being surrounded by other people who also think big and want to do great things. It is difficult for me to find words to describe how great it feels to be in that position, to be in the company of those kinds of people, all of us in pursuit of a common goal. The secret is that we still focus on the basics. We just do them better than anyone else.

My primary job as the leader of my company has been to develop a core team of people with this special ops mindset. Most of them have never been in the military let alone special ops, yet each of them has developed an exceptional way of approaching and solving problems. That is why we have managed to have such an outsized impact in the cybersecurity realm. Even so, we really need capable backup in this David versus Goliath battle we are waging. We need fresh horses. That is where you come in.

< >

Now that we know the environment, the enemy, and ourselves, I must ask: Do you believe that the problems outlined in Part I are unsolvable, or someone else's problem to solve? Or do you believe, as I do, that we—meaning you and me and our fellow Americans—can and must reject the status quo, band together as a special ops unit to fight this asymmetric war and win it, and successfully defend our way of life?

If your answer is not a "Hell, yes!" then it is a no. Total focus is the only way to solve really hard problems like this. We have to be fully engrossed and completely on purpose at all times. The remainder of this book lays out the groundwork for that. Whether you are fighting a cyber war or trying to solve any other tough challenge in business or life, the special ops mindset and techniques I teach you here will help get it done.

PART II

CONNECTING PEOPLE TO THE PURPOSE

- **Special ops truth #1:** People are more important than hardware.
- **Special ops truth #2:** Quality is better than quantity.

When something truly nefarious goes down—such as the massive FireEye and SolarWinds hacks in 2020—you cannot expect to assemble a bunch of the best minds in a matter of a couple of weeks and figure out a broad-spectrum solution to resolve it. Put another way, you cannot mass-produce a capability after an emergency. By then you are behind the power curve.

This is the hard lesson the United States learned in 1980 in the conventional realm with our failed attempt to rescue fifty-two American hostages from Tehran during the Iran Hostage Crisis. The reason the Operation Eagle Claw mission failed was not because the hostage rescue element personnel were not capable of doing their part. It was because of politics and a lack of integration. Every military service wanted some level of participation in the operation, so they hurriedly cobbled together a response that included them all. They employed air force planes whose pilots were not used to landing on desert landing strips. They had navy ships whose crews were not accustomed to launching those kinds of special operations from their vessels. They sent Marine helicopters with pilots who were used to flying over the jungles of Vietnam. Because of all the dust in the landing zone, one of the choppers hit a plane and caught on fire, and the whole thing went downhill from there. The mission to rescue the hostages was ultimately aborted.

Although the mission itself was a failure, something good did come out of it: we established a joint special operations task force that brought together all the services to train, equip, and work collectively *before* a crisis emerged on the ground. We learned how to establish a small group of plank holders charged with helping build a bigger team with the right set of skills, constructing what ultimately is a platform of the basics that can be taught quickly and uniformly to future team members. Remember: the basics do not exist until somebody creates them; that is the job of the plank holders.

Interestingly, the term "plank holder" originally referred to an individual who was an inaugural member of the crew of a United States ship or Coast Guard cutter when that ship was placed into commission. Today the term is used more broadly to apply to individuals, in military or in business (or engaged in any critical operation/mission in life), who are there from the inception of the project and thus who are critically integral to its design, formation, and direction. That is precisely my meaning here.

But how do you draw the right people into something that has no brand and get them to build from the ground up the foundation for the basics? Especially when those basics are going to go against conventional wisdom? How do you find—and prepare—the right people when the problems they are intended to address are incredibly complex and insidious, such as fighting a war in the Fifth Domain, or going up against a major business competitor who will stop at nothing to beat you, or cleaning up the oceans, or (fill in the blank with whatever asymmetrical David versus Goliath problem you are facing)? How do you attract those people, connect them effectively to your purpose, and convince them over and over again that this effort is a good use of their precious time, energy, and intellect?

This is the topic of the next three chapters. Once you have mastered the techniques outlined here, you should be able to say with clarity that you and your teammates have a near certain probability of (1) doing cool things (2) that make an impact (3) with people you like.

CHAPTER 4

DOING COOL STUFF

All men who feel any power of joy in battle know
what it is like when the wolf rises in the heart.

—Theodore Roosevelt, *The Rough Riders*

Blackness. Sweat dripping down my face, all the air ripped from my lungs. I lay motionless surrounded by pine needles and frozen dirt melting into mud. Seconds passed that felt like an eternity as I gasped for breath and regained my vision, looking up through the pine trees with the sun's warmth on my face. Kevin ran up to me and asked if I was okay. As I struggled to say, "I can't breathe," he smirked. I can see the look on his face as vividly today as I did more than fifteen years ago. His response: "If you can talk, you can breathe."

It was my first week in special operations and my first time on one of the most challenging obstacle courses there is. In transition from a lateral rope around a tree and onto a platform, I stepped on a piece of old tire rubber that had been bolted to the tree. It gave way and I hit the corner of the raised platform as I fell to the ground. As I laid there with the wind knocked out of me, the pain I felt was nothing compared to the thought that my tenure in the world's most elite unit would end before it really began.

The basketball-sized bruise on my ribs hurt, but before it had faded, I was back on that O Course. This time, however, Kevin was told to actually show me the proper technique.

While factors like practice, luck, upbringing, and/or genetics are important when it comes to performance, there is no substitute for knowing the proper technique. It is why in Brazilian jiujitsu there is the common practice I allude to in a previous chapter of pairing new students who have a size, strength, and weight advantage with light students of advanced technical skill, preferably a woman if one is available. It is not intended to embarrass the new guy—although that is frequently the effect—but rather to prove the superiority of the proper technique regardless of other factors. All things being equal, technique wins, and in many cases the better technique wins even when all things are *not* equal.

As you are building your team of plank holders who will run your selection process and teach new recruits the proper technique, most people will not have the exposure, experience, or details to fully understand the intricacies of an unconventional, complex, risk-focused, systems-based approach to problem solving. You cannot afford to recruit individuals who fit a profile perfectly for each role and function. That is traditional wisdom, and it has failed in cyber warfare as it has in many other domains. Following traditional, conventional means of recruiting results in only getting those dissatisfied or disillusioned souls you can profile, target, and pitch. You also cannot win by incentivizing people with a fabulous work-life balance, extra pay, more time off, or, for the love of God, the ping pong tables and sleep pods that you see some organizations use. Those are the tools of the well-funded or well-established, and candidly, they do not motivate the kind of people you need at this stage. Those things may work in a conventional approach. Conventional approaches—manifestations of experience, repetition, structure, and control—are how we get to the Pareto Principle, which is a level of waste that special operations leaders and those historical figures I most admire have rejected. They do not lead to strategic efficiency.

But your first cohort has to come from somewhere. There is good precedent for pulling candidates who have the right mentality and mixing the backgrounds and skills to build out a pool of resources for future selection. The CIA started with the Office of Strategic Services (OSS) as its foundation, and the OSS started with people recruited from the Ivy League. First Special Forces Operational Detachment–Delta started with individuals drawn from the special forces community and based on the lessons Colonel Charles Beckwith learned from the 22 SAS (British Special Forces). The Naval Special Warfare Development Group (NSWDG) was formed from the Navy SEALs.

You have to draw from established sources, but it is not the strongest advocates of conventional success that you are looking for. You are looking for those individuals who see all of the flaws in bureaucracy, who see the limitations of the conventional approach. You are looking for the disruptors, the architects—those restless souls not satisfied with the status quo. They are the ones with high learning agility, emotional control, and a healthy distaste for dead weight. You are looking for people who believe that *building is better than transformation*. People who are willing to reject and tear down the traditional systems and practices they were exposed to previously but do it in a reasoned way that can be broadly understood.

To get people who are willing to both think that way and give it their all, you must draw them in first. You have to make what you are planning to do seem cool to them. "Cool" is wholly dependent on the individual, but you have to make your mission look and sound cool and then find ways to continually connect them back to the purpose. That is where it makes an impact. They need to feel that there is going to be a tangible outcome, they must believe in the purpose that you have articulated, and then they need to feel like the traction they are making is going to ultimately result in achieving whatever the core mission is.

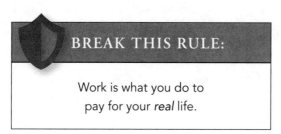

BREAK THIS RULE:

Work is what you do to
pay for your *real* life.

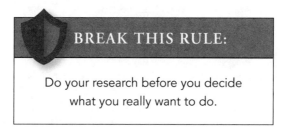

BREAK THIS RULE:

Do your research before you decide
what you really want to do.

BECAUSE IT LOOKED COOL

Blue liquid dripping off my face into the ragged sink inside the shop. My reflection in the dirty mirror—a line delineating the placement of the mask and goggles. I had spent the previous eight hours under a large boat sanding the bottom paint off, the fine blue powder showering over me. I decided in that moment that my lot in life was not going to be a life sentence. Days later I walked into the recruiter's office to get a conditional release from the National Guard, where I was scheduled to attend helicopter mechanic school in September of 2001, so that I could go active duty and leave sooner. On April 17, 2001, I drove my 1983 Toyota

Corolla to the Military Entrance Processing Station, tossed my keys to my sister, told her she could keep the car, and walked away knowing that she didn't even know how to drive a manual transmission.

I was on my way to One Station Unit Training to become a 54B Chemical, Biological, Radiological, and Nuclear (CBRN) Operations Specialist. I picked CBRN because Reconnaissance sounded cool in the book that outlined all the army's various jobs and associated specialties. As I waited to be in-processed, I looked up at a poster of badges and medals and told the sergeant there that I wanted Recon, Airborne, Air Assault, and Military Freefall—not as a request but as an objective.

"If Recon or Airborne isn't in your contract, you won't get it," he replied flippantly. "Air Assault is the hardest two weeks in the army, and Military Freefall is only for Special Forces."

Whatever, bro, I thought. *I'm going to get them. All of them.* At that point, I had no idea what any of those things actually entailed or what it took to get them. But they looked cool, they sounded cool, they were perceived to be challenging, and this guy said I couldn't do it—all the necessary and sufficient ingredients to motivate me.

Four months later, I was in my second day of the CBRN Reconnaissance course—which I had gotten by request after being named Distinguished Honor Graduate of the CBRN Specialists course—when planes flew into the Pentagon, the World Trade Center, and, thanks to some courageous passengers, a field in Pennsylvania. A large-scale terrorist attack against your country has a way of messing with your plans. I had figured I would crush through some things, get a degree, and then perhaps go Special Forces or become a helicopter pilot, but when September 11 happened, I had to adapt to the complexity of doing all of that while at war. Time was not on my side. I graduated from the CBRN Reconnaissance course in mid-October and went straight to Fort Polk, Louisiana, without taking leave. A couple weeks later, I turned eighteen.

I was not at Fort Polk long before I learned that there was an Air Assault school on the base and that all the people my company sent kept failing. So, in my infinite wisdom, I bet my company commander that I would not only pass the Air Assault course but also get Honor Graduate—asking, if I did, for him to get me one of the brigade-level slots to Airborne school. I won that bet, and my company commander kept his word.

In the spring of 2002, I departed for my first deployment in the Middle East as part of Combined Joint Task Force–Consequence Management (CJTF-CM) as a CBRN Reconnaissance Specialist with a nineteen-ton M19 Fox reconnaissance vehicle and both Airborne and Air Assault wings on my chest. For the next three-plus years those wings helped me stand out from the crowd, get promoted quicker than I would have otherwise, and get the missions and assignments I wanted. Yet I did not jump out of a plane or engage in a helicopter assault the entire time.

THE MODEL FOR ELITE TEAM BUILDING

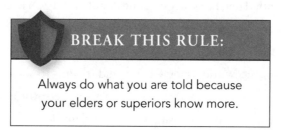

BREAK THIS RULE:

Always do what you are told because your elders or superiors know more.

In response to all the hijackings that were happening in the 1970s, Colonel Charles Beckwith founded the Delta Force in 1977. Taking what he had learned in the British Special Air Service and as a special forces officer during the war in Vietnam, he was determined to apply a different approach to dealing with this adversary that was not the Soviets of the

Cold War era. He had to fight against the conventional wisdom of other special forces organizations and old-school military generals to get the organization established, but he prevailed. Because of his tenacity, some of the most significant military victories we have had since the late seventies have been achieved through the efforts of this small organization selected from all the other military services and then trained to execute things that most people would consider to be impossible. His book, *Delta Force: A Memoir by the Founder of the U.S. Military's Most Secretive Special-Operations Unit*, inspired me to jump at the chance to join special operations, where I spent my formative years from age twenty-one to twenty-six. The team-building skills I learned during those five years have served me well in every aspect of my life.

One of the most important lessons I learned from my time in special operations is that elite teams are first and foremost self-selecting. Selection has to be difficult and take potential team members beyond the typical scenarios they may find themselves in mentally, physically, and emotionally. You do not want people discovering their limits when everything is on the line. It also must be consistent, such that people of diverse backgrounds, skills, and experience can be assessed against the same standards. This is less about equality, equity, fairness, and so on than it is about necessity—because that provides you with the greatest potential for diversity of knowledge, skills, and abilities while creating a formidable common bond for those who make the cut.

First, you have to find a way to draw the right people to the cause, and that means that the cause has to be cool. To solve hard problems, it is necessary to gain the interest and inspire the passions of those who could do anything else they wanted. So, let's set the scene: you have people who are successful in their roles—they have high potential for upward mobility in a world that celebrates the value of a conventional approach and a standard progression path. And what are you offering them?

Mostly, uncertainty. The work will definitely be hard. Success will not be acknowledged. Failure is potentially catastrophic. Instructions? Nope. You are going to have to figure it out on your own, on the fly. Sounds great, right?

If this does not sound cool to you, then you passed; you are probably normal. Most people do not like ambiguity and spending every waking moment thinking about all the ways bad guys could do bad things. Most people are not attracted to the idea of jumping out of "perfectly good" airplanes. I get that. If you are not into the former, there are plenty of other causes for you. If you are not into the latter, never get into a plane used for skydiving. There is nothing "perfectly good" about them.

At this stage you do not have the luxury of tolerating team members or plank holders who will not do whatever it takes. You are going to have to break ground to build; to cut a path without knowing what is behind the brush; to sacrifice time, blood, sweat, tears, and so much more. You have to both *be* these people and attract these people without the luxury of movies, books, and stories of exploits—both successes and failures. At this point, you have two primary recruitment tools at your disposal: *framing* and *symbolism*.

MAKING THINGS COOL

Getting the support of potential plank holders for your mission is not easy. It is a process of trust building, positioning, and a bit of the nexus between preparation and opportunity (a.k.a. luck). Connecting the gut instinct about the problem you want to solve and the data you are allowed to communicate to candidates is a bit like untying a knotted-up fishing line with one hand. So, how do you communicate, at large scale, that your purpose is cool and that exceptional people should connect to it, especially when they do not fully understand what it is you're doing?

You start by employing *symbolism*: using icons—words, images, people, marks, locations, or abstract ideas—to represent something beyond their literal meaning. The symbols you use have to align with something that your target population already feels is cool. With our customers, we call this "known demand."

> **BREAK THIS RULE:**
>
> Presenting the situation how you envision it in the future (and not how it currently is) is misleading.

For example, to recruit people to special ops, the military uses posters and videos showing members of the command doing cool stuff like jumping out of airplanes and coming out of a swamp carrying a rifle with night vision goggles and a scuba mask on. They don't tell you that the man who is coming out of the swamp looking like a badass is scared to death that a poisonous snake is going to bite him on the face, or that he has been in that water for five hours and has never been more miserable in his life. They fail to mention those things. Does not matter. That guy looks cool!

Remember Rosie the Riveter? She was the symbol of the strong and capable working woman during World War II, when the U.S. government needed all hands on deck. American women viewing her image back then probably had no idea of all the sacrifice that would be required to work on behalf of the war effort in dirty factories and dangerous shipyards while simultaneously and singlehandedly raising a family, but hey, Rosie looks cool, so sign me up! Decades later, Rosie remains an enduring emblem of tough, independent women. That is symbolism at its finest.

Framing is the way your message is communicated. It means giving accurate information that is intended to enable an audience to take the next logical step without knowing all the details. When I am trying to recruit people to support my company's mission, I don't say, "We look at known threat intelligence and indicators of compromise, and then we place technologies that generate logs, extract the data from the log sources, and generate correlations to identify events." That is too much detail. It is beyond most people's technical comprehension, so I have to frame it such that they will understand what they need to understand so that they can connect the dots in a way that makes sense and matters *to them*. I ask them pointed questions, much like Leonardo DiCaprio's character, Jordan Belfort, did in *The Wolf of Wall Street* when he challenged some sales executives to "sell me this pen." If you are not familiar with that scene, Google it. If you want to dig into it further, go to YouTube and search for "Jordan Belfort sell me this pen" to hear it straight from the horse's mouth. You will learn that the sales process is not about saying how cool the pen is, because one guy's cool pen is another guy's boring pen. Making it cool to each potential buyer requires a customized approach—an analysis, an inquiry.

When I am trying to "sell" my company's mission to potential plank holders, teammates, and customers, I start by asking questions: *What are you passionate about? What are you exceptionally skilled at? How do you want people to remember you?* Once you understand what this person needs and values, you can construct the perfect frame for them. You can tell them a story about your mission that circles back to their definition of cool and helps them connect to it on an emotional level.

Not everyone is going to be so tuned in to your mission that you can get technical with them. They will come from diverse backgrounds. They may be salespeople, other executives, consultants, junior staffers, and even volunteers, all of whom will need to go into a technical training

FRAMING AND SYMBOLISM

In this context, *framing* is the packaging of an element of rhetoric in a way that encourages desired interpretations and discourages others. For political purposes, framing is about presenting facts in such a way that implicates a problem that is in need of a solution.

Symbolism is a literary device that uses icons—be they words, people, marks, locations, or abstract ideas—to represent something beyond the literal meaning.

program before they can begin to understand even a smidgeon of what you are doing. They may be your customers, partners, and clients, who will ultimately be consuming a capability you are bringing to the table to force-multiply so you can have the level of impact you are trying to achieve. That is why your mission has to be framed in a way that people can take the next logical step and believe that the next logical step is cool, unique, differentiated, and effective.

I wrote my master's thesis on framing and political discourse, and the example I used was how our government framed the Iraq War. What did the top four figures in the executive branch—the president, vice president, secretary of state, and secretary of defense—say leading up to and during the Iraq War to get people to buy into the mission? What I found was that the vast majority of their claims—essentially that Saddam's a bad guy, Saddam has weapons of mass destruction, and Saddam won't let inspectors in to verify what he's doing over there—were factual.[17] All

---

17   See, e.g., Colin Powell, "U.S. Secretary of State Colin Powell Addresses the U.N. Security Council," February 5, 2003, https://georgewbush-whitehouse.archives.gov/news/releases/2003/02/text/20030205-1.html; George Bush, "Transcript: George W. Bush's Speech on Iraq," *The Guardian*, October 7, 2002, https://www.theguardian.com/world/2002/oct/07/usa.iraq.

those statements created a frame wherein the pundits and the American people took the next logical step and came to the conclusion the executive branch hoped they would: "Saddam's a bad guy who's got weapons of mass destruction that he won't let us monitor, and he's going to use them against us. Go get him!"

Another example is the mission to end the plague of alcoholism. When Alcoholics Anonymous launched, they needed to assemble a set of plank holders who would serve as counselors and sponsors to provide support to the membership and train more counselors and sponsors as the organization grew. They started by promoting the message that alcoholism is detrimental to society. It is unhealthy and causes crime and death, but if you are suffering from it, you're not alone; we will help you get sober and stay that way (the frame). Millions of people took that message to the next logical step: *if AA had been around when I was a kid, my dad might have put down the bottle and not destroyed our family; if AA had been around when we were teenagers, my best friend might not have been killed by that drunk driver.* These people did not need to understand precisely *how* AA would achieve its mission. As long as they were personally connected with it, they were on board.

Long after the recruitment of your plank holders is done, you will continue working to keep them and the rest of the team engaged. The use of symbolism and framing never stops. It will not be the same as it was in the beginning because your people will have more information as time goes by, but you will still have to guide them, over and over again, toward taking the next logical step.

Now think: What symbols can you begin using today to help potential plank holders connect with your purpose and discover for themselves how cool it is? How can you frame your mission in such a way that people cannot wait to make it their own?

CHAPTER 5

STUFF THAT MAKES AN IMPACT

We have real enemies, dedicated to dominating and eventually destroying us, and they are not going to be talked out of their hatred.

—Lieutenant General Michael T. Flynn,
"The Military Fired Me for Calling
Our Enemies Radical Jihadis"

Whenever we are facing a really big problem—terrorism, transnational crime, human trafficking, global infectious disease, weapons of mass destruction, or, in our reference case, cyber warfare—it is easy to articulate that the issue is important. Importance without progress, however, breaks the weak team members quickly and tires those with grit eventually. What is left, after a time, are only the fanatics—those who are operating on emotion or insanity (as the saying goes, doing the same things over and over again but expecting different results). This is why all challenging pursuits, especially those that demand the absolute best of us, require a regular show of progress, wins, or a clear demonstration of achieving an impact.

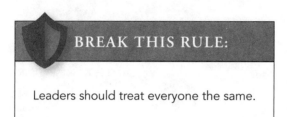

BREAK THIS RULE:

Leaders should treat everyone the same.

Have you heard of 4ocean? It is a business whose purpose is cleaning up the oceans, rivers, and coastlines. They know that having random groups of volunteers do sporadic trash cleanup on the beach will not be enough to get the job done worldwide. The problem is so big that it would be really hard for those who support the mission to see the progress and feel the impact they are making. Eventually even the most resilient and caring volunteers and workers will give up. So 4ocean found a way to demonstrate progress through recognition of their supporters' contributions and acknowledgement of small successes along the way. They provide this recognition in a variety of ways that serve to reward and motivate their volunteers and supporters. For example, they designed bracelets—a visible sign—that supporters can buy with the promise that for every bracelet sold, the 4ocean crews stationed around the world will pick up one pound of plastic from the oceans. Knowing that other supporters would prefer to see the actual data, 4ocean legitimized their progress claims by partnering with the Better Business Bureau to audit and verify their progress, which is publicly reported every quarter. Now, supporters who fund the company's activity by purchasing a bracelet have a tangible connection to the impact, and the people doing the work have an authoritatively verifiable measure by which they can say they have achieved some semblance of success.[18]

Like cleaning the oceans, the long cyber war we are in today—mostly

18   4ocean, "About," accessed February 28, 2022, https://www.4ocean.com/pages/about.

unbeknownst to the average American and largely unacknowledged by many "in the know"—incremental impact, wins, and recognized progress are critical to keeping the warriors from succumbing to battle fatigue. If they think that cyber stuff (or whatever big problem you are trying to solve) is cool but they do not believe it is possible to win, then all they are thinking about at that point is how to make the most money. Stated somewhat differently, if something is cool (or simply feels that way) but does not make an impact, then it will at best be a hobby and not a calling or a cause.

KEEPING THEM ENGAGED

Once you have gathered your core group of plank holders, your job as the leader is to constantly keep them connected to the purpose. You have to keep them winning by creating achievable milestones, acknowledging progress, and celebrating even the smallest of victories. It sounds so basic and simple, but if it is, why do so few leaders do it? I think it's because we "executives" tend to be so deeply and passionately connected to all aspects of the problem we are trying to solve. We imagine that everyone around us is equally immersed and can also see the value in what we have done, or what we yet need to accomplish. That is rarely the case. We have to look for creative ways to bring folks back to the *why* over and over again and acknowledge their efforts every step of the way.

The ranking system in jiujitsu gives us a prime example of how this works. Everyone starts as a white belt in jiujitsu and works toward the blue, purple, brown, and ultimately, the black belt. It is exceptionally challenging to become a black belt. Very few who start will ever make it that far. Actually, it is a challenge to earn anything beyond the white belt. It takes years for most people to get to blue, and then they generally quit. Of the blue belts who go on to earn the purple, most will stick with it as long as family, kids, work, and health concerns do not derail them. Almost all who make it to brown continue on to black.

In an effort to keep people training and engaged in jiujitsu, there are degrees (a.k.a. stripes) that practitioners earn between the belt promotions, which serve to help them feel like they are making progress. They have to feel like the hours they are putting in are making them better. It is tough for most people to feel that way since they lose in training all the time. Rewarding them with stripes and belts brings them back to the belief that their effort is having an impact even if they do not realize it. Can you really say that a three-stripe white belt is better, even incrementally, than a two-stripe white belt? No. It is incredibly subjective. But that stripe you put on that person's belt may be the thing that keeps them dedicated to their training. Not just in the short term to get to the next stripe but in the long term to eventually become a black belt and contribute back to the martial art. The belts and stripes are symbols and celebrations of progress, of impact. They motivate practitioners to continue taking the next logical step in their pursuit of excellence.

In similar fashion, the military awards good conduct medals every three years as well as achievement and commendation medals. The public acknowledgment that one did something of value is enough to keep most people going. The big impact you are trying to achieve may be winning the war, but you can't get everybody connected to that very broad, diverse, and intellectually complex conceptual outcome. You have to keep them connected to the progressive outcomes that they personally have some control over and that make sense to them.

In my company, I use a variety of techniques to reward and acknowledge the people on my team. All the traditional motivators are there. Some folks are inspired by being entrusted with the hardest assignments. Others get pumped up by a personal visit and an acknowledgment that we have heard good things about them and their work. Much like parenting and romance, individuals have unique languages that they align or resonate with. As a leader, you have to know and understand those languages *and use them*. As long as people feel like they are making tangible steps and can start having visibility into the outcome, then those who have the right stuff will stay engaged.

FANATICS NEED NOT APPLY

When someone is fifteen hours into work that is not sexy *and* they do not feel like they are making any progress, it is easy for them to give up. Nobody will bang their head against a wall forever.

> **BREAK THIS RULE:**
>
> You need the most passionate people on your team because they breathe energy into the cause.

The conventional wisdom in modern politics is that you want fanatics on your side; the more, the better. They are the ones who donate money, attend meetings, man the phone lines, and wade through snowdrifts to knock on doors and pump up the electorate to generate more fanaticism for the movement. But what the fanatics also do is push the other side of the political spectrum such that we end up with a battle of fanatics on both flanks with the rest of us in the middle, shrugging our shoulders and shaking our heads. Fanaticism does not accomplish anything of value, and collateral damage is the real impact.

World War II gives us a good case to examine here. Prior to the attack on Pearl Harbor, we were supporting our allies quietly, but the official position was that it was not our war to fight. In some cases, U.S. citizens fought for the allies—some pilots went and joined the British Air Forces—but the country as a whole was not mobilized. It took the shock of Pearl Harbor to do that. If it takes a crystalizing event like Pearl Harbor or the exploitation of fanaticism to mobilize us—those being the two primary historical catalysts for broad spectrum engagement in conflict—then we are at a massive disadvantage. The crystallizing event means that we would allow a fundamental change to our way of life before we would be compelled to move, while the fanaticism-leveraging approach loses steam quickly. Wild-eyed fanatics will not enable you to win because they cannot separate from the emotion, the othering, the good-versus-evil mentality. They are so caught up in the drama, they can't see straight.

Contrast that with the unconventional special ops approach to team building that I am advocating. As explained in Chapter 2, to beat the adversary, you have to be able to evaluate them with a clear head and put yourself in their shoes. Fanatics simply cannot do that. In the cyber arena, we are playing chess on the global stage. The last thing we want is for our opponent's next move to cause us to fall into a trap. It is easy to induce a team of fanatics to have an evoked response because they are an emotive audience. I see this play out all the time in jiujitsu, which is basically just a game of human chess. Or put differently, you could think of your opponent as a 200-pound Rubik's cube that you are trying to solve. In my matches—especially against an opponent who I sense might be driven by emotion or otherwise not properly evaluating the situation—I will often give up a dominant position to induce him to enter into a trap that I've created to force him to submit. Fanaticism opens up opportunities for traps in much the same way. Before you know it, the mob starts driving the problem-solving effort and the leader who was trying to play chess is suddenly in the midst of an anarchistic free for-all-that he or she cannot control.

So I do not like having fanatics on my team. They may bring a lot of energy but they do not bring the level of self-discipline to consistently make good decisions and logically evaluate the adversary's moves so we can counter them (and hopefully play some offense rather than always being on defense). I want people beside me who are cool and calculating. People with grit and a steady hand. Then I give them enough symbolism, framing, and realization of impact so they can continue the fight when it ceases to be fun. Not only will they build on what will become the basics, but they will also bring like-minded people onto the team.

CHAPTER 6

DOING STUFF WITH PEOPLE YOU LIKE

I'd rather go up the river with seven studs than one hundred shitheads.

—Attributed to **Colonel Charles Beckwith**

I joined 1st Cavalry Division as a young sergeant with two deployments under my belt and a double stack on my chest. (A "double stack," for the nonmilitary reader, means I was privileged to display both Airborne and Air Assault badges on my uniform.) My wife at the time was pregnant with our first child. All she had known since our marriage was my departure and brief return home, which involved a seven-month stint and included a move from Louisiana to Texas. The company I joined was rolled into a Field Artillery Battalion, which was in turn rolled into the 5th Brigade Combat team of 1st Cavalry Division. At that point in early 2004, it barely mattered what your military operational specialty was. We were all going to do the same thing.

BREAK THIS RULE:

Personalities do not matter as long as
everyone is respectful.

I was only in the company for a matter of weeks before I was on a plane headed back to Iraq. I was just twenty years old. But with nearly sixteen months spent in combat zones between Operation Enduring Freedom and Operation Iraqi Freedom, I was one of the most seasoned combat leaders in the company and had the most recent and relevant experience in what we were doing. And my next mission turned out to be a lesson about what can happen if you fail to recognize that it is often the case that personalities *do* matter.

As we arrived for the departure ceremony, I had already flipped the switch. I was in deployment mode and the presence of my pregnant wife crying in the car was a distraction from what I needed to do. I had soldiers under my charge who were not particularly inspiring. Our leadership (if you can call it that) was in many cases (but not all) an unhealthy combination of scared and incompetent. My peers were more concerned about who they would enroll as their "deployment spouse" than accomplishing any mission.

We finished the ceremony, loaded up, and departed for the airport. As I walked up the stairs onto the plane, one of the squad leaders from another platoon decided the impending shit show was not for him and sprinted—as best he could—down the tarmac. I never figured out what he was thinking; nor did I ask. He still ended up coming but did so as an E-5 instead of E-6. (An E-5 is a sergeant, one rank below an E-6 staff sergeant.)

When we arrived in Kuwait, it was a familiar scene for me. I had driven those roads for most of 2002 as a member of the CJTF-CM and again in early 2003 as we waited to invade Iraq. We loaded up on familiar buses and embarked on a familiar route. As we departed Kuwait International Airport en route to Camp Virginia, I pulled back the shades, viewing the strip lights that bracket the open terrain of the Kuwaiti desertscape. Behind me, one of the Field Artillery guys freaked out. I scoffed at his outburst. As if the large convoy of buses leaving the airport escorted by Humvees with automatic weapons manned by young men and women in U.S. Army camouflage could be anything other than the next crop of troops heading north. At the time I thought he was a scared, inexperienced jackass. In hindsight, perhaps I was desensitized by a lifetime of experience, recent familiarity with the environment, or a mindset that could easily be characterized by an overwhelming sense of calm. My youthful perspective put a fine point on what I was dealing with.

We would be in the desert on the Kuwait side of the berm for weeks. The deathly heat was already setting in as we went through training on close quarters battle, convoy operations, and so on. The quality of training was abysmal in comparison to what I would eventually experience, and the logistical faux pas still sits in the front of my mind.

Prior to deploying, the command ordered sights for our weapons, scopes, flashlights for mounting, and lasers. It was as if they watched a special operations movie and ordered everything they saw. They spent thousands of dollars on every soldier, preparing us for the evolution in combat operations that was taking place post-invasion. However, they failed to account for the fact that our M16A2 rifles lacked the rail system that would allow the gear to actually be used. Read that again. We each had thousands of dollars' worth of critical tools that we could not use because we lacked a twenty-dollar adapter. I ended up taping a flashlight to the barrel of my rifle. In the grand scheme of things, it did not matter, and it was not the last hack we would do to get the job done without the right gear or techniques.

When the time finally came to push north, I was the vehicle commander (VC) for an LMTV (a type of light utility truck) with no armor. We crossed the same border as I had the year prior during the invasion, but this time, rather than being in a Fox reconnaissance vehicle with a driver I trusted looking for weapons of mass destruction, I was paired with someone who had to try three times to pass the entrance exam to get into the army and appeared to suffer from narcolepsy. It was a struggle to keep him awake and avoid crashing into the vehicle in front of us as we made our way north to the base on the southern edge of Baghdad. The kid, as I reflect on it now, was probably older than me and had no business being in the army, let alone on this deployment that would see much of my platoon wounded in the Mahdi uprising driven by Muqtada al Sadr.

As we made it into the base and began clearing weapons, the lack of effective training and preparation came into stark focus. One of the privates negligently discharged his rifle four inches from my foot. Not surprisingly, our platoon sergeant put all her attention on accountability for our basic load (210 rounds of ammunition). People went as far as taping their magazines to avoid losing rounds. That BS lasted for only a few days. It all changed once we got out on the roads.

The first major ambush happened on Route Senators. An RPG was fired from the right side of the road in the alley between two apartment complexes while our patrol was conducting route clearance operations. The RPG hit the trail vehicle with our platoon sergeant in it and nailed the seam on the right rear door. The blast was directed inward and sprayed shrapnel and flame into the cab, catching one of our troops on fire. I jumped out of the lead vehicle and ran back looking for the point of origin, and when I couldn't ID the assailant, I transitioned to getting everyone off the X. I passed the platoon sergeant as she ran past me screaming, "My baby is on fire!" The young specialist driving the vehicle was in shock. She could not figure out how to get the vehicle to move, so I yanked her out. I put it in park, verified that it was still operational, restarted it, and got it into drive as we called for the Quick Reaction Force. We evac'd the injured kid and returned to the base—a four-hour patrol that lasted forty-five minutes. That was one of the last missions that this particular platoon sergeant and driver went on, and it was only a couple of weeks into a thirteen-month deployment. Ours was the opposite of an elite team.

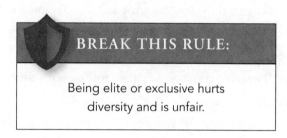

BREAK THIS RULE:

Being elite or exclusive hurts
diversity and is unfair.

There is nothing wrong with being elite. Elite organizations are inherently diverse, but the intangibles go much further than that. Truly elite organizations are self-reflecting and self-selecting, have high levels of accountability, and drive toward resolving the most difficult and worthwhile challenges. They know why they are there, and they lift each other up when the work stops being fun. They trust one another so much that they are willing to bail out a teammate without question to get the job done.

I'll give you a real-world example from my own company. This occurred at a time of year when we are typically trying to close out a bunch of deals; there is a massive amount of activity around that. One of my key team members in pushing our deals through is a woman I will call Eva. I have multiple conversations with Eva almost every day about how those deals are going. A lot rides on her shoulders to the point that she rarely gets any time off during this period, and when she does, she's almost always interrupted. She never complains about it, though. She is that dedicated to our mission and everyone in the company knows it.

Sadly, Eva lost her father a year ago. He was her hero, and his death was devastating. As the one-year anniversary of his passing approached, Eva became withdrawn and had a little trouble focusing. I knew what was on her mind, but not everyone else did. Still, nobody questioned anything. They rallied around Eva and carried the weight for her without a single grumble or mumble or complaint. For Eva, having that experience, having her colleagues show her that trust and compassion and lift her up when she needed them, was hugely comforting and inspiring for her. It actually inspired the whole team because we recognized that if any one of us were ever down or unavailable for some reason, our teammates would carry us through, with zero trash talk.

If you do not have that, if you don't have people around you whom you like, who are connected to the purpose, and who care about you, your environment will become toxic. At that point everyone is just working for the money, not working toward the mission.

Eventually, what the elite team is doing stops being about the symbol, the idea, or even the hatred of the adversary. What it boils down to in the end—when things get really hard—are the people to your left and to your right. They are the force that will see you through. Stated somewhat differently, when you are on an elite team doing really challenging things, there is no higher meaning or conceptual driver. This is a concept aligned with the hierarchy of needs. The "cause" is tertiary to the people you are with.

HUNTING WHERE THE DUCKS ARE

When I was in the process of joining the army, I read Colonel Beckwith's book and that led to the goal of joining special operations when I was old enough to go through selection—the minimum age was twenty-two—so it came as a surprise to me when, at age twenty-one, I received a cryptic email from someone in special operations asking if I was interested in doing something different. I was in Baghdad for my third deployment at the time. When I returned stateside, I went through the process and, as you already know, I was selected. They waived the age requirement for me, making me among the youngest members in the history of the SMU.

People often ask me how that organization found me; how did they know I might be a good fit? I do not know for certain, but my guess is that they discovered me through profiling via the army's human resources management system. They searched the database for high achievers (similar to what we do today in the civilian world through LinkedIn), and my name kept popping up. My scores on the vocational aptitude battery were high, especially the General Technical (GT), which assesses your ability to do different vocations. If you score above 110, as I did, it is an indicator that you have the capacity to do any job in the military. That might have attracted them right off the bat. They may also have liked that I had been the distinguished honor graduate of all the schools I had attended. I was already Airborne qualified, I had reconnaissance training, and I had multiple deployments, a Purple Heart, and an Army Commendation Medal for Valor. I met the rank requirement (sergeant or above), I exceeded the minimum PT test score average, and I had completed the primary leadership development course. All of that earned me the opportunity to go through assessment and selection for my first job in special operations.

Finding the right people is key. In what unconventional places might you find folks with the diverse skill sets you will need for the core competencies that will become your basics? Once you have identified that and have the principal group of plank holders established, you can then use those plank holders to crowdsource the rest of the team. Thus, you're pulling from a broader audience of people with high learning agility, acumen, emotional stability, and intellectual capacity. You then train them on your basics and turn them loose to work their magic. It does not really matter where they come from. Over time their previous experience, even if it does not have direct applicability to what you are doing, will infiltrate your mission and make the whole team stronger. A solid selection process and a good training program are collectively what it takes for people to fully grasp and execute the basics, and in the process form a world-class team whose members trust and support one another as they go about the business of doing cool stuff that makes an impact.

Trust and support among teammates are important no matter what your mission is, but they are critical when the task at hand is ultra-challenging. Imagine that there is a guy named Carlos whose mission is doing rescue climbing. When Carlos was a kid, he thought mountain climbing was cool; that is why he got into rescue climbing in the first place, but he stuck with it because of the impact it makes. Let's say that somebody is trapped on the side of a mountain and Carlos's team has a five-day climb to reach them. By the end of the second day, Carlos comes to the conclusion that he can't trust one of his teammates to get the next hook in, and the other two guys are a couple of whiners. Carlos will finish that rescue, but he is not going to do it again with that team. He will take his talents and skills elsewhere.

The lessons from this short fictional anecdote should be clear: If it is not cool, they are not going to be drawn to it. If it does not make an impact, they are not going to stick with it when the going gets tough. And even if it is cool and makes an impact, if they are not surrounded by people they like and trust, they will quit—or simply leave for somewhere else.

You do not come to the idea that you are going to change the world overnight. Long before movies and books are made about your success, and long before people view your company as *the* place to work, you have to gather together the plank holders who will bring the right ingredients to the table. You are selecting them based on of their ability to decompose the long-term solution and extend it to other parties through their grit and their cultural fit. That is your starting point. Those people will then bring in the next layer of the ecosystem—the additional human pieces of the puzzle. You will vigorously assess, select, and ultimately down-select some of those candidates. By the time you get to this point, down-selection is predominantly due to fit. Since the candidates were so carefully targeted and assessed by you and your plank holders, you know that they have the right background and skills to get the job done. It all comes down to cultural fit—do they have it or don't they? If they do not—even if they are high performers—you have to let them go, even at the risk of creating a negative perception. The good of the organism is far more important than the performance of its individual organs.

It has been my experience that when you hit the mark with selection, the people you are surrounded by give you an incredible sense of ease. Again, I return to the analogy of the rescue climbers. If you know the people to your left and right are the best in the world at what they do and you would not want to be doing that job with anyone else, it gives you the mental and physical capacity to go far beyond your perceived limits and feel comfortable doing it.

Even to this day, when I get on the phone and talk to one of the guys that I worked with in my formative years, I feel better. Instantly. It does not matter what we are talking about. My blood pressure drops, and I relax. It is a weird thing for a barrel-chested freedom fighter to say, but it is almost like sitting around a warm campfire wrapped up in a favorite blanket. Those guys give me a level of comfort that makes me want to excel, and that inspires me to make better decisions so I can go further, faster, and harder.

The same thing happens when you get it right with your plank holders. If you do not get it right, you will end up with fives hiring fours and fours hiring threes because there is a lack of confidence; everybody's concerned about retaining their position. They do not want to hire somebody who is a threat to them. When that happens, you will know it. You will see your team getting nowhere fast because there is no one capable of pushing you forward.

I want people to come into my company and be better than me. I wake up every day with the goal of working myself out of a job. I am not saying that I am hoping to be replaced. I am saying that my job is whatever the company needs from me on any given day, and I have to figure out how to work myself out of that job so that either it can be done successfully by somebody else or it becomes unnecessary. Eliminate, simplify, automate.

And then? Scale it up.

< >

Part II centers on articulating a broad vision, using unconventional means to grab and focus a small, diverse team of key plank holders. Their role is to master and then teach the basics to even more people with the right stuff. This gives them the necessary tools to create forward momentum. Once you have done that, it is time to scale it out to have a meaningful impact.

One way of looking at scalability is to think of a virus attacking a cell. As the virus, your goal is to displace all other properties surrounding one aspect of your problematic cell and cause it to burst in order to release more virus to infect other problematic cells. (Can you tell that I wrote this book during a pandemic?)

Put another way, to solve this hard problem, you as the leader must enable the initial plank holders and the people they train to proliferate the broad spectrum of response that is needed to build resiliency in your mission.

PART III

UNCONVENTIONAL AT SCALE

- **Special ops truth #3:** Special operations forces cannot be mass produced.
- **Special ops truth #4:** Competent forces cannot be created after emergencies happen.
- **Special ops truth #5:** Most special operations require non–special operations forces support.

E lite organizations have an outsized impact on challenging problems. Elite individuals have an outsized impact on organizations. We saw it during the troop surge in Iraq in 2007. Embedding a couple of operators in an infantry company exponentially increased that company's impact. Not because of optics, intel, halo infiltrations, or cooler guns, but because the application of *unconventional outcome-based thought processes* eliminated the unnecessary and simplified the important. It is a basic concept—challenging convention—to achieve the outcome. I am not exaggerating when I say that it has saved my life over and over again.

So how do you use your core team of plank holders as a hub and create spokes to mobilize a broader audience, much like the JSOTF did for the infantry during the surge? That is the subject of Part III.

CHAPTER 7

MISSION AS A CONCEPT

Let us go forward in this battle fortified by
the conviction that those who labor in the service
of a great and good cause will never fail.

—Attributed to **Owen Arthur**

I n the introduction I relate the story of my Alive Day—the story of the night my unit was ambushed on a dark and dusty road in Iraq. I would like to circle back to that event here. If there is one thing I learned from that ambush, it's that sometimes, doing "the right thing" is not the right thing to do. If I had followed my training on the conventional way to react to an attack like that, to drive through it, I and many of my fellow soldiers would be dead today. No doubt about it. Making the hard decision to throw out the rule book and act in direct opposition to my training is the reason I survived and was nominated for a Bronze Star for heroic action in a combat zone. As my Alive Day story illustrates, the conventional and right action is usually the predictable action. The predictable action is exploitable by your adversaries. Being exploitable is how you get pwned.

Perhaps, like me, you understand the predictability-exploitability connection, so you have no qualms about breaking the rules to get the job done. Maybe you have even gone so far as to form a core group of people you like, your plank holders, who are also ready and able to use unconventional means to do cool stuff that makes an impact. Now you have to take this concept of unconventionality and scale it so that even more people understand what the right thing is to do, and then based on all the data points they have available to them in any given moment, summon the nerve to pivot toward what will actually work so you can win. To do that, you have to package the mission as a concept.

DRIVING HOME THE POINT

When I was trying to find my initial group for Conquest Cyber, I looked to my customers and my competitors. Who was already trying to solve this cybersecurity problem on an individual level? Those people became my pool. And then, within that pool, I looked for those disenfranchised souls who did not feel like they were ever going to make an impact where they were. Those folks became my targets. When I was having a one-on-one conversation with each of them in an attempt to connect them to my purpose, the data points I was taking in were generalized. I was responding not only to what they said but also to their body language. I knew what I was trying to accomplish, I knew the big problem I was trying to solve, and I knew that I needed additional skill sets and other people around me who believe the same things I believe. I found those people and connected them to the purpose using framing and symbolism.

BREAK THIS RULE:

Always hire the candidate who best
meets the qualification requirements.

Next, my plank holders and I had to find more people to round out
the team—people who had never touched any of this cybersecurity stuff
before. At that point, I no longer had the ability to get belly-to-belly with
everybody who crossed the transom in order to move things forward. I
was not going to see the eye twitch or the shifting in the chair or hear
the tone of voice of every single candidate. I was not going to be able to
detect all the subtle cues that let me know how my message was being
received. I had to conceptualize our mission in a way that answered all
the data points for people on a broader scale so that I, using my plank
holders as the hub, could draw in every race, creed, color, nationality, and
so on. People with degrees from Harvard and people with no degree at all.
I knew that if they were connected to the mission in their own personal
way, they would bring a level of diversity of solution that was ultimately
going to make everything we were doing better as we grew from a small
group of plank holders into a much larger network of capability. And
now we are engaged in extending that network of capability outward ultimately to mobilize the whole country to be able to respond effectively to
the cyber challenge we are facing.

To achieve that worthy goal, I created a simple conceptual analogy so
that everyone on my team, from the freshest-faced newbie to the most
battle-scarred veteran, can connect to the mission, understand their role
in it, and measure their own individual progress. I have conceptualized
the mission in this way because I found that the people I cannot be face-
to-face with every day were seeing the assorted elements of our mission

in isolation; they did not comprehend how all the various threads connected. I had to turn the mission into a concept that they and our wider audience could wrap their minds around even if they did not understand all the details. Here is what I came up with:

Conquest Cyber's Mission as a Concept

- Compliance → maturity → effectiveness = our pathway, or *vehicle*
- Eliminate, simplify, automate = our approach, or *engine*
- Product-integration-outcome nexus (PION) = our guiding principle, or *GPS*
- Ensuring cyber resiliency for our way of life = our *destination*
- Doing cool stuff that makes an impact with people we like = our *fuel*

Let's break this down. Compliance, maturity, and effectiveness make up a *vehicle* the team and individual team members use to know where they are at in the process of getting our clients protected. If a client is not yet compliant with laws, standards, or regulations, you have to put your head down and attack that first. If they are compliant but the compliance is not yet mature (meaning that they are not conforming every single day), then we have to get that done. Once they have hit maturity, the next logical step is effectiveness: enabling them to do what works 365 days a year. This is the approach we use in building capability for our clients. We get them compliant, institutionalize the compliance to make it mature, and then focus on ensuring that their cyber programs are consistently effective at preventing or mitigating their specific design basis threats (DBT). DBT is a term I have adapted as a set of individual threat profiles that we use to build each client's cybersecurity program.

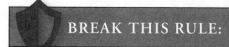

> **BREAK THIS RULE:**
>
> Prepare for the zombie apocalypse
> and you will be fine.

Many people believe that as long as you prepare for the worst possible circumstance—what I like to call the zombie apocalypse—you will be covered for anything. Others are so acutely (myopically) focused on their particular area or expertise that they think it is the only thing that matters. Both mindsets are completely ineffectual at winning in the complex world of cybersecurity. In fact, they are off base if you want to solve *any* big, complex, enduring problem. Using the concept of DBT, you start to filter the noise and nonsense, enable articulation of complex threat scenarios, and facilitate a risk-focused, systems-based approach to improving resiliency, mitigating vulnerabilities, and monitoring threats with enough time and resources to adapt to an ever-changing battlespace.

All along the way, our vehicle of compliance, maturity, and effectiveness is driven by the *engine* of eliminating everything we do not need, simplifying everything we do need, and automating everything possible. Eliminate, simplify, automate; that's our underlying mantra, and we are downright merciless about it. We have eliminated more than 70 percent of vendors associated with our technology infrastructure, simplified our approach to underlying security architectures, and automated compliance, program maturity, maintenance, and testing for cyber program effectiveness against our DBTs.

Our vehicle's *guide* or *GPS* is the product-integration-outcome nexus, or PION. What is the way forward for each individual and the various functions of our organization? In the absence of order, what do they do? Some in Conquest are focused on the product, some are focused on integrating technologies, and some are focused on achieving the outcome, but we are all charged with ensuring that those three converge so the outcome is delivered through integrated technologies and enabled through our products. In the absence of clear guidance or a task list, those responsible for the outcome try to drive that outcome into closer alignment with the product and the integrations. Those responsible for integrations are focused on enabling those outcomes via the product with exceptional ease of use. All are responsible for thinking about how their daily work drives us closer to a seamless overlap between our product, the integrations that support it, and the outcomes that we are trying to achieve.

Our *destination*—ensuring cyber resiliency for our way of life—is the mission and the purpose. That mission is so clear that all people regardless of background, experience, and perspective can embrace and further it, even when their comprehension of the "why" is different than mine.

And finally, our *fuel*: doing cool stuff that makes an impact with people we like. As I learned in my formative years in special operations, when everyone is connected to the purpose and committed to each other, nothing can stop you.

This simple concept of vehicle, engine, GPS, destination, and fuel can be applied to just about any complex endeavor you can imagine. It allows people to embrace something they do not fully understand. It allows them to get past "othering," the conventional and perilous trap of thinking in terms of good versus evil. As we learned in an earlier chapter, when you are thinking in those terms, you cannot get inside the adversary's head and understand their thought processes. You cannot beat them. In the cyber realm we have, acting against us, literally the entire world, whether they be current state enemies, nonstate terrorist organizations, unreliable and potentially ineffective allies, or just plain neutral actors. We have gone from being the Goliath superpower to putting ourselves in a position of being a David. David cannot win by meeting Goliath on his own terms, or by just trying to defend against the giant's persistent and unending attacks. That would wear David down in a hurry.

Here the old saying applies: *They only have to be right once. We have to be right every time.* When you conceptualize your mission so that anyone can connect to it and embrace it regardless of their background, their industry, or their role, you are well on your way to being right—and doing right—every time.

CHAPTER 8

GRIT AS A KEY DIFFERENTIATOR

There is no God-given right to victory on the battlefield.
You win that through the skill and the devotion,
the valor and the ferocity of your troops.

—**General James M. Mattis,** quoted in Andrew Tilghman,
"Retired Gen. James Mattis Says Civilians
Know Little about the Military"

The first selection process that I went through for special operations happened right after a thirteen-month deployment with the regular army in Baghdad. A few weeks after I got back to the States, they flew me to Fort Bragg and took me through a full day of intellectual, physical, and psychological testing. At the end of the first day, we did a road march. Road marches in the army are commonly twelve miles long with a rucksack on your back. This one was eighteen and more of a "ruck run" given the limited time to complete it. It was pretty grueling being in poor shape from deployment and after many hours of testing, but I made it.

Afterward, I got in my rental car and took off for my hotel. I was so tired that I fell asleep at the wheel before I even got off the base. I awoke to the sound of sirens and the glare of flashing lights in my rearview mirror. It was an MP pulling me over to ask me why I was doing eighty-five miles per hour in a forty-five-mile-per-hour zone. After talking to me for a few moments, he came to the conclusion that I was not a drunken speeder but a completely exhausted special ops candidate. He let me off with a warning and a bit of friendly advice: pull over and get some sleep. I drove to the parking lot of a fast-food restaurant just outside the base and slept for a couple hours before continuing on to the hotel.

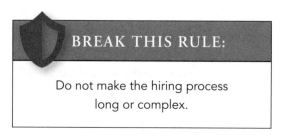

BREAK THIS RULE:

Do not make the hiring process
long or complex.

The next morning, I returned to base for more of the selection process. They drove me out to a spot where there were ropes tied between three trees that were each separated by about twenty feet. The ropes were maybe five feet off the ground and parallel, and the objective was to use the ropes to make it to the end without touching the ground. They had a guy show me one time how to traverse the course and then it would be my turn. He jumped on and started swinging around on the ropes like a monkey, making it to the end in less than a minute. He made it look incredibly easy. Turns out, it was probably one of the most difficult physical exercises I have ever done. I was hanging on and inching from one rope to the other using every muscle fiber I had left. I was completely smoked—had no grip strength left—but I made it without falling off. It took me close to fifteen minutes that felt more like an hour. I felt an incredible sense of accomplishment, but it was admittedly pathetic in contrast to what I would be doing in the coming weeks.

Next, they loaded me up and took me to what looked like a sewer pipe sticking out of the ground, its diameter just slightly wider than my shoulders. This tunnel was actually a maze inside—a series of pipes and dead ends—and I was ordered to make my way through it. I peeked inside and found that it was pitch black in there. My first thought was rattlesnakes and whatever other kinds of creepy crawlers I might encounter in there. It did not matter. I had to go. I crawled through, feeling my way around until I came out on the other side.

Then they took me to a room filled with pieces of strange equipment and manuals sitting next to each one. They told me that they were going to leave me there for fifteen minutes and when they returned, I would be required to give them a class on an item of their choice. There were about thirty things in there and I had never seen any of them before. The handlers left the room (but still observed), and I went to work skimming the manuals, learning the names of these pieces of gear and the basic functionality of what they do. As promised, my handlers returned in exactly fifteen minutes and selected the item they wanted me to present: a piece of radiation detection equipment. Using the little bit of information I'd gleaned from the manual, I gave my presentation, such as it was.

At the conclusion of that exercise, they told me that I had to plan a mission to take down a suspected enemy facility. They gave me a big piece of butcher paper, a marker, a list of the resources I had available to me (a group of advanced infantry, some operators, and a group of specialists) and set the clock for ten minutes. I sketched out the mission, the timer went off, they came back in, and I briefed them on my plan. That was the last activity of the day. During this whole time, the only words that were ever spoken to me were the instructions for each exercise and "Follow me" each time they led me to the next challenge.

The next day I went before a board that consisted of some stakeholders, some unit members who were not part of this specific troop, and an operator named Pat. Pat was the deciding vote and happened to be the same Selection Sergeant Major I mentioned earlier. Recently, I learned that at the end of the interview, Pat told those assembled, "If you don't take him, I will."

They took me. Three months later, I was running that selection process.

That was when I learned the rationale behind the organization's selection exercises and assessments. I discovered that it all came down to identifying who has grit. Can you adapt and be flexible under pressure, or do you break? Can you think logically when you have no specific guidance on what to do? And can you keep going even when 99 percent of the population would quit?

The baseline expectation for every person in an elite organization is grit. In this SMU it did not matter if you were a CBRN guy like me, a sniper, a mechanic, or a cook. You had to be able to think logically and make good decisions when you did not have all the data. You had to be willing to keep going even when things got hard—in fact, *especially* when things got hard. This is the yardstick by which I helped select new members, and it is the way I measure everyone who wants to join my company today.

THE ASSESSMENT THAT NEVER ENDS

Let's imagine that you have got your plank holders in place, you have conceptualized the mission to the point that most people can wrap their minds around it, and now you are being overrun with folks interested in joining you. You cannot accept (or retain) everybody who comes through the door, or you will end up with a major logistical challenge without the level of follow-through it takes to accomplish anything of significance. This is hand-to-hand combat characterized by deep inter-personal interactions as you guide, coach, teach, mentor, listen, and work together to try and build a successful organism. If you just let that organism replicate without putting some level of control on the selection and retention processes, ultimately efficacy will suffer, and your organization will cease being special and unconventional. You, or your organization, will just be fat. Like special ops, you need a way to test for the one characteristic that sets the warrior apart from the wannabe: grit. Grit is your key differentiator.

To communicate this truth to the people in my company, I created a set of core values I call DELTA: drive, excellence, loyalty, teamwork, and adaptability. The first four values are a low enough bar that most people can align to them fairly easily. It is the final one, adaptability, that breaks people most often.

The inability to adapt when faced with a tough obstacle quickly erodes the other four values. When someone is put in an uncomfortable position, the first thing that happens is that their capacity for *teamwork* starts to dissolve. When they fear they cannot do a task, they lose the *drive* to continue. They do not even want to try because they do not know the specific steps they need to take to achieve *excellence*. Then, if they are uncomfortable and they lack grit, their *loyalty* evaporates, and either you will have to let them go or they will select themselves out of the game.

It does not matter if every member of your team has drive, excellence, loyalty, and teamwork. What matters is whether they are able to retain those qualities when circumstances become difficult, or when the people themselves become uncomfortable with the unfolding situation. Can they *adapt* and *innovate* when the next step is uncertain? Will they continue to carry the torch when faced with an immense and unfamiliar challenge, and the pain that likely comes with it? That is the true test of their value as a member of the elite team.

Your selection process has to allow you to rapidly identify who has the grit, the stick-to-itiveness to be able to follow through when the work gets really hard. When it starts being real. When it takes thirteen hours a day for six months to get your system protected from the bad guys. When you have to go through every bit of code, line by line by line, looking for potential back doors and exploits. You have to do that day after day after day after day, knowing that if you are wrong the impact could be disastrous, even catastrophic, and if you are right there is not going to be a celebration in your honor. There will be no accolades for stopping an attack. There will only be punishment if you do not. Because that is your job.

If you do not build grit as a baseline of expectation within your selection process and your retention, laziness will creep in. People will give up and you will lose your fight. But how do you select people for grit? How can you tell who has got it and who does not?

You test them on it, plain and simple. You test them over and over again until the weak ones fall away and all you have left are the badasses. Find out who will break before the enemy does. The enemy always gets a vote.

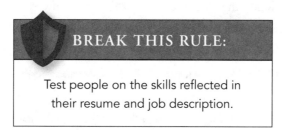

BREAK THIS RULE:

Test people on the skills reflected in their resume and job description.

Selection was grueling, but the assessments did not stop once we were chosen. Our leaders found all kinds of imaginative (some might say merciless) ways to keep finding out what we were made of, to try and break us—or perhaps, to strengthen our resiliency. I recall a lengthy and particularly difficult training mission in which we flew on air force planes to multiple sites doing different types of operations: conducting infiltrations, taking down various kinds of targets, and rescuing hostages. It was a marathon, ten-day training exercise during which we slept on the ground whenever we had a spare moment, planned all day, and did missions every night. We were so ready for it to be over. Finally, the day arrived to go home. We boarded the plane, the aircraft took off, and we exhaled. Only then did we receive word that there was an operations order for us to leave for another mission as soon as we arrived back at the base. Our expectation of being able to drop our gear, go home, and get a good night's sleep was dashed in an instant. We thought we were done, and now this? We were furious. I am not ashamed to say that I almost fell apart. Almost.

That was the point. Our leaders planned it that way. They wanted to see who among us would break. Better to have an operator break between missions than during one. None of us broke that day. We had been selected for grit and we proved that we still had it. At the time I did not understand why it was important for us to always be forced to exercise that grit, but now I know: there is a level of resiliency that comes from that experience of being tested. It is like getting inoculated. You get inoculated in training for what you are going to face in combat. People fall to the level of their training; they do not rise to the level of their potential.

THE "SOCIAL EXCUSE" AND OTHER TESTS FOR GRIT

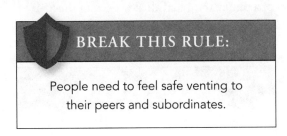

BREAK THIS RULE:

People need to feel safe venting to their peers and subordinates.

It is not only about selecting people who have grit and make good decisions under pressure. It is also about selecting people who will maintain morale. If one person is allowed to start complaining that "this is bull-shit," which is what happens in the regular army and in conventional circles, it has a negative effect on others who might also be feeling the pressure but otherwise would endure. That is why you must have or engender those elements that I talk about in Part II: doing cool stuff that makes an impact with people you like. When you are a leader or plank holder in an elite organization, chances are you all believe in what you are doing, and you are with people you like. In that case, your core group can avoid ever getting to a point where someone poisons the well by saying "this is bullshit."

However, as you scale up from ten to one hundred or more, you may no longer have that deep level of trust that permeates your core group. If you allow any negativity or what I call "social excuses" to creep in, your organization will devolve in a hurry. People will break right at the moment when it's most important that they endure.

I saw this happen all the time when I was undergoing operator selection. There was one incident I will never forget. A bunch of us operator hopefuls were sitting around talking about our current jobs during a break from our grueling mountaineering and advanced land navigation test. I listened to one guy go on and on about how much he enjoyed his current assignment in Okinawa. It was great! He loved it! He had it made over there! This got my attention. Remember: I was only twenty-five years old and kind of a punk, and I had already been in the SMU for four years. I could not resist the opportunity to mess with him a little.

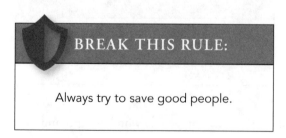

BREAK THIS RULE:

Always try to save good people.

"Well, if you've got it so good in Okinawa, why the hell do you want to do *this*?" I asked. "I mean, why do you want to give up a good thing to go through this shit, killing yourself climbing these mountains every day only to be at the bottom-of-the-barrel in the organization—*if* you're even selected?"

The next morning when we woke up, that guy was gone. He had packed his things in the middle of the night and slunk away into the darkness. It never failed: whenever I ran across an operator candidate who had the mindset that he was already happy with what he was doing, all he needed was a social excuse to quit—which I always gave him as an assessment of his grit—and the next day he was history.

Humans are social creatures. If you allow the social excuse for mis-aligned behavior to exist, it metastasizes and ultimately erodes what you are trying to accomplish, especially if it's something as big and significant as winning a cyber war. You cannot allow those people who lack grit to be a part of your scaling process. You have to select people for grit, and if they start to show cracks in their ability to maintain it over time, they have to go. It does not matter if they are the smartest person in the room. It does not matter if they are your highest performer. It does not even matter if they are the smartest person in the room *and* your highest performer. If they demonstrate a lack of resiliency when things get hard, they are going to end up providing the social excuse for quitting to their teammates who would otherwise endure.

A good test for grit is to put people in uncomfortable positions and see how they react. As soon as somebody appears to have a sense of what their tasks are on a day-to-day basis, move them into a different part of the organization. In other words, it is up to you as the leader to not let people get too cozy, to give them responsibility for new and challenging things and then see how they handle the opportunity. If Mike seems to value titles and having a number of people under him in your organizational structure, move him into a strategy role where he's acting as an individual contributor. If Lucy appears to only want to be an individual contributor, move her into a role where she has to manage other people. You will quickly learn who can do what it takes when you need them—at those most critical moments when you really need them to do what it takes.

> ### BREAK THIS RULE:
>
> Put people in the role they are best suited for and get out of their way.

I recognize that this is the opposite of the conventional leadership approach of getting the right people into the right seats, giving them their tools, and then leaving them alone and letting them do their thing. That may be fine in a typical setting. But in an elite organization, you can shake things up because you have the plank holders there. You have the core built out and you have created enough demand, enough desire for masses of people to want to participate in what you are doing. You are essentially allowing people to scrape their knees but not letting them drive out into oncoming traffic. If you just hold the bike for them and leave the training wheels on, they will never get better. They will never learn about equilibrium, anticipating the moves of other vehicles or pedestrians, or leaning into turns. You do not want them to feel socially uncomfortable or feel like they can't ask questions. You just want to shake them up a little bit and see what they are made of. If they truly have the right stuff, they will thank you for it later. If they do not, at least you will know before any real damage is done. The important thing is this: The only people who do anything of consequence are those who are constantly learning and evolving.

I am a prime example of how stretching, whether it is self-imposed or forced, can make one's life so much more interesting, impactful, and fulfilling. To be clear about this, let me explain that by "stretching" I mean taking an individual skill and pushing the envelope of its limits, or more broadly, taking a set of skills from different areas of expertise and applying them to new and potentially unique challenges. As I was getting medically retired, I was in a job in the Defense Threat Reduction Agency. I could have stayed in the government forever doing emergency management, figuring out mass warning and notification systems at military bases, and assessing plans, among other tasks. It was an important job helping to protect against terrorist attacks, school shootings, and the like. But it did not challenge me. It was so un-challenging that I was able to do the job full-time, go to graduate school full-time, and still be bored.

As I transitioned out through medical retirement, I took a job coordinating national-level response exercises to weapons of mass destruction. I was figuring out how to break into nuclear missile silos, having people jump out of airplanes, and doing sniper shots and live fire exercises. The position allowed me to stretch my political muscle too because I had to get approval from governors and base commanders to do things that they otherwise were not comfortable doing, such as detonating 300 pounds of explosives out in the middle of fields in Montana and Wyoming. That was fun, but it was also not very challenging.

Next, I took on global pandemics. I led a program that responded to the Ebola outbreak in Sierra Leone and climbed around attics in Kazakhstan collecting bat samples. I trained former Soviet scientists on how to safely collect samples and do genetic analysis to discover new viruses. I wrote a book on disease emergence from the Asia-Pacific region in 2015. That job stretched me, challenged me, and the work was interesting and important, but it was not with people I liked. Some in the organization hated the military and hated the fact that their company was getting money from the DoD. The culture and vibe did not align with me. It was like the scenario I presented earlier about being a rescue climber and not trusting the people to your left and right.

Then, on a jiujitsu mat shortly after moving to Florida, I met a man named Gerard. The story he tells is that I nearly broke his back that day, but I tend to focus more on what happened between us off the mat in the months that followed. We clicked instantly, and the more we learned about one another, the more we realized that we are kindred spirits when it comes to our willingness to follow unusual paths to get the toughest jobs done. Gerard is one of the owners of a leading technology company, and he hired me to expand his company's offerings from the private sector into the federal government and its industrial base. With Gerard, I knew that I would have the freedom to do cool things that made an impact with people I really liked. It was literally the difference between night and day compared to the company I had been with previously.

All the uncomfortable stops and starts I had endured in my life made it possible for me to do the vital work I get to do today. Had I remained in my easy job as an emergency manager, I would never have had the honor of becoming the president of a rapidly growing cyber risk management firm that puts all my skills and talents to the test every single day. I have taken the combined experience of emergency management, project management, information security, red teaming, managed security, and cloud security, along with the intangibles of knowing how to navigate politics, to build data analytics software that is the solution for one of the most pressing problems we face in America today.

As we scale our organizations unconventionally, we need to offer our people the same kinds of opportunities for growth that I just described. We let them bring us their diverse experiences, and then we put them into positions where they can gain new ones. The only way to do that is to shake them out of their comfort zones and test their grit on an ongoing basis. Remember: like special ops, your elite organization is not necessarily hunting for the quickest, the strongest, the best looking, or even the smartest people. *You are looking for the people who will not give up or abide stagnation.* That is the key differentiator.

CHAPTER 9

CULTURE AND BRAND AS A CATALYST

Your brand is what other people say about
you when you're not in the room.

—Attributed to **Jeff Bezos**

A few weeks into writing this book, I read a news story com-
memorating the seventeenth anniversary of the capture of
Saddam Hussein by the Fourth Infantry Division and the
JSOTF. The story mentioned the infantry division first, but everybody
who was involved in the mission knows that it was actually the JSOTF
that got Saddam. The JSOTF used the infantry as enablers because the
infantry had the big armor and the people to support it. So why would
the Fourth Infantry Division support the JSOTF instead of just doing
their own missions? It is because there's a powerful brand associated with

the JSOTF: it is recognized worldwide as an ultra-elite military unit. That brand is a catalyst, not just for drawing the right people to the cause but also for drawing those who will be needed to support the core group when it becomes necessary.

Brands are inherently fragile. Organizations spend massive amounts of money and time developing and trying to control their brands, and equally large sums trying to tear down the brands of adversaries and competitors. Strong brands require cultural alignment—the kind of cultural alignment that is rooted in shared experience and substantive verification—by (1) those within your organization, (2) those trying to join, and (3) those you want to inspire to support you from the outside.

If there is not an elite brand associated with your organization, you will not be able to draw the support people you need on the battlefield once you start to scale this out. Consider the cybersecurity arena. The way our war in cyberspace is transpiring, there are assets we are going to have to buy and assemble, processes we are going to have to implement and change, and pivots we are going to have to make as we engage in this combat, and all of that requires support. To get the companies, research institutions, utilities, governments, and everyday Americans to embrace our approach and align with us, we need a strong brand. I cannot think of a single business, organization, or movement that would not benefit by having a more robust brand. How do you build a brand that is strong enough to become a catalyst?

FORMING THE CATALYST WITH YOUR TEAM

You have conceptualized the mission to where others can embrace it and do something with it without you having to be so close to the nucleus of how the problem is getting solved. You have selected people with grit and brought them into the fold. All things being equal, you have chosen those who have endured hardship and demonstrated the ability to overcome obstacles. Those are the ones who are going to be there with you in the trenches at three in the morning. You have given them a baseline of tools, trained them, and tested them for grit on an ongoing basis. Now you can start to see a culture form around the who, what, when, where, why, and how of your mission. That culture, that brand, is what ends up attracting and keeping the best possible talent.

Again, special ops provides a case study in how branding can be a vital catalyst. Every day for my first four years in special operations, I drove past a five-story building with open windows, an internal staircase, and a wall with nothing but some external piping spanning from the bottom to the top. I often saw snipers practicing from the roof of this building, and occasionally I ran up the internal staircase carrying five-gallon water containers for physical training. One day I asked a mate who had been in the organization a couple years longer than me what the wall with all the exposed piping was for.

"People free climb that," he replied.

My evoked response was, "Are they nuts? You'll never catch me doing that!"

You see, despite the wings on my chest from Airborne, Military Free Fall, and Air Assault, and after multiple combat tours earning Bronze Stars, a Purple Heart, and an Army Commendation for Valor, I was and am terrified of heights.

For three years after learning what that wall was used for, I pondered it every time I drove by or reached the rooftop with my five-gallon water cans. *It is crazy that people climb that wall! There is no way I would ever do that.*

One morning I walked into the bay and checked the schedule posted on the board to see where my group was headed that day (I was the designated one of the Troop Sergeant Majors responsible for getting my people to and from wherever they needed to be, complete with the right gear), and what I read stopped me in my tracks. Our mission was to free climb to the top of the five-story building. In true special ops fashion, our instructors provided the specific directives that would allow me and my team to scale the wall safely, and minutes later I found myself cresting the top of the building that I swore I would never climb. My leaders believed that I could do it even though, over the course of the previous four years, I had not. Most importantly, from the founding of that SMU until that fateful moment when I received my order to climb that wall, they had fostered a culture that would not allow me to hesitate. I would literally have rather fallen off that building than hesitate.

That SMU's culture is a two-way street: when you are asked to do something, you do it, *and* you do not ask people to do dangerous things that you have not given them the capability and resources to do safely and effectively. It is the whole grit thing being constantly and consistently reinforced. That was the culture that created the brand, which ultimately is what proliferated and got those of us in the organization to a point where we could do daring things that others would consider to be magical. When you are told and shown repeatedly that you can always do more, you begin to lose sight of your limitations. There was not going to be anyone else to call when it was time to get things done, so we had to use any means necessary to figure it out. That is when you start exploring the art of the possible with your team.

In my company I am always scouting for ways to inject that elite, no-holds-barred, no hesitation brand into everything we do. I want my people to know without a doubt that they are fully equipped—mentally, emotionally, intellectually, and physically—to scale any wall, no matter how high. They will know this because they understand that I have selected and retained all of them for their grit and given them the training, the capabilities, and the trust to make it to the top.

FORMING THE CATALYST FOR ASPIRING MEMBERS

Once you have established a strong brand for your internal team, it is important to communicate that brand to those on the outside who may want to join you. Remember that they can come from anywhere; they do not necessarily have to be immersed in your world already. In the instruction phase of SMU selection, for example, candidates come from various backgrounds. Obviously, you have to be smart, have emotional stability, and have proven yourself capable of performing in other conventional or special operations capacities. There is a general belief that if you are successful in selection, you will also be successful in the organization. However, beyond those basic expectations, the candidate pool is wide open.

The way the selection process is run is a monument to that organization's culture and brand. The impact of that is that everybody who is chosen for that team has the mindset that when they are told to go scale a five-story building, they are going to do it. They are going to know that the people to their left and right are going to do it, too. Those who do not make it through selection come out of the experience with the perception that this organization is the top tier—these guys are the best in the world. In other words, everybody who goes through the selection process, whether they are chosen or not, comes away a believer in the brand.

There are a couple of ways that special operations perpetuates that outcome. The first is to re-baseline everybody at the beginning of the selection process. It does not matter whether you are a special operator from the navy, air force, marines, or army or a CBRN guy like me. It does not matter whether you have been through two combat tours or ten. Everything you need to know to be successful in selection is taught to you in selection, and the way they do that is notable because it reinforces the brand. Surprisingly, the teachers during the instruction phase are not seasoned veteran operators like you might expect, but junior operators. They bring everybody into the classroom and start communicating the critical blocks of instruction that everyone needs to know to be successful, and they deliver it perfectly without any support. No notes, no PowerPoint presentations, nothing. Just a young guy standing up at the front of the room and flawlessly delivering one-hour blocks of instruction on complex subjects like advanced land navigation, without the aid of notes or technology of any kind. All of it off the top of his head, without any emotion, without error, sweeping the room from left to right, doing what takes most professional teachers or speakers years to master. The pressure on them is immense—forgetting one small detail that the candidates need to know could potentially cause everybody in that class to fail—yet I have never seen or heard of one of them stumbling.

Imagine the effect of seeing these guys, many of whom had been sitting in your very seat less than a year ago, being able to pull that off? For the candidates who are selected, the effect is the realization that *this is the level of professionalism that is expected in this culture*. For those who do not make it, which is the majority of the people in the room, it is the realization that *this is the level of professionalism that is to be emulated*. That is what they are going to tell everyone about their selection experience, including potential future special operators. That is the brand as a catalyst being spread one degree out from the team and then, ultimately, even further out to the people who make up the next layer: those outside special operations who may be needed to support them in the future.

FORMING THE CATALYST FOR THE BROADER AUDIENCE

Most people will never attend special ops selection or even know somebody who has. Of those people who do attend, most will not make it.

Only a handful of individuals will ever experience what it is like to be in an SMU even among the military population, let alone the country at large. That is just the reality. So how is it that so many people know that Special Forces, Rangers, SEALs, or any of the other elite units are cool? How is it that there are some units whose very existence is classified yet millions of people still know about them and consider them to be so incredibly badass that it inspires them to want to join the military themselves, or at the very least provide support for those organizations without question?

The way that jiujitsu became popular in the United States offers a clue. The first Ultimate Fighting Championships (UFC) were won in the early 1990s by a guy named Royce Gracie, one of the least well-known members of the prominent Gracie martial arts family of Brazil. Royce, 170 pounds soaking wet, went into the UFC and beat fighters who were more than twice his size. That started folks talking and recognizing the capability of jiujitsu and ultimately led to the growth of the art. Americans flocked to Brazil to study and then came back to the United States to open schools. The word spread, and it became a movement of sorts. Jiujitsu was soon recognized as one of the best martial arts in the world and has since become an integral part of the military and special ops combatives programs. These days, every MMA fighter must know the concepts of jiujitsu, if not be an advanced jiujitsu practitioner.

It is the same with any good brand. If it is interesting and trustworthy enough, word spreads outward like the ripples on a pond, and the brand touches people who were nowhere close to the place where the pebble hit the water. That is what happened with special operations. Recall Chuck Norris's 1980s movies, *Blackhawk Down*, and the television show *Six*? Even nonmilitary types could not resist. Over the years, some details about these organizations got leaked out in the press, and pundits expanded on that, piquing the public's interest even more. Also, some people wrote articles and books about their experiences in the culture. For example, the unit's founder, Charles Beckwith, wrote his memoir, *Delta Force*. Former operator Eric Haney wrote *Inside the Delta Force* and found himself *persona non grata* after it was concluded that he revealed too much sensitive information. And General Stanley McChrystal wrote *Team of Teams: New Rules of Engagement for a Complex World*, in which it was disclosed that the JSOTF was responsible for the 2006 death of the leader of Al Qaeda in Iraq, Abu Musab al-Zarqawi. Even the president acknowledged that it was SEAL Team Six that killed Osama Bin Laden. Much was said about the elimination of these particular targets because of their responsibility for untold numbers of brutal killings, including the beheadings of innocent people.

All those things—the books, the movies, the video games, the leaks—end up creating the brand, the legend. That is why the Fourth Infantry Division was more than happy to support JSOTF in capturing Saddam. The way you get what you need when you need it is by having a stellar brand.

My experience has been that when you are operating at that tip of the spear, for lack of a better term, there are not very many of you. You need the help of tier-two people who have adopted some of your tactics, techniques, and procedures. The close-quarters battle (CQB) methods that operators generated through constant training, assessments, and missions, for example, has spread from the tip of the spear out to the larger pool of special operations folks (the Rangers, special warfare crewmen, air force tactical air patrol, etc.) and ultimately into the broader military force. Now, some truck driver moving cargo from Kuwait to Iraq is being taught CQB fundamentals for clearing buildings that were originally developed by the most elite units. This creates scale without making everybody a special operator. It drastically enhances the capacity of the entire movement.

That is what I'm talking about from a business branding standpoint. If you think your brand is just something your marketing team creates for you, you are making a costly mistake. The internal culture is the foundation for the brand, and minus a strong brand as a catalyst, you cannot achieve broad-spectrum adoption of your cause. The effectiveness of the culture enables the brand to create scale as it generates a movement that, while it does not completely replicate your tier-one capabilities, improves everyone else's. It is the rising-tide philosophy in action.

PART IV

THE GUY ON THE GROUND

It is not the critic who counts; not the man who points out how the strong man stumbles. . . . The credit belongs to the man who is actually in the arena . . . who strives . . . to do the deeds; who knows great enthusiasms . . . who spends himself in a worthy cause; who at the best knows . . . the triumph of high achievement, and who at the worst, if he fails, at least fails while daring greatly.

—**Theodore Roosevelt,** speech at the Sorbonne, Paris, April 23, 1910

W hat is the role of the leader in the unconventional, elite organization? I would argue that the substantive difference between "the leader" and leaders in general is insignificant. It is to provide purpose, direction, and motivation to accomplish the mission.

Purpose has been the subject of the first three parts of this book. In this context, however, purpose is less about *the* purpose and more about *their* purpose. Personalized and functional-level purpose. Now we are dealing with a created ecosystem in which people's individual experience and inclinations influence the perspective and comprehension of the overall purpose. Purpose—when highly contextualized to the individual—provides clarity, comprehension, and consequence.

Direction is another topic we have given some attention to. The context here is through empowerment. Where you want to be versus dictating the route. I have a simple philosophy when it comes to direction: do what is important and urgent. Once those are done, find a way to work yourself out of the job.

Toward that end, I have broken down my business and my leadership role into four main areas: build, expand, deliver, and enable. This is how it looks for my company:

- Cyber strategy and product development = Build
- Strategic development (sales, marketing, partnerships, alliances, etc.) = Expand
- Cyber risk and cyber operations = Deliver
- Talent management, compliance, legal, contracts, finance, and so on = Enable

The next three chapters cover these concepts in depth, highlighting the functions of building and enabling the team at scale—focusing on being better at the basics than anyone else. I cover the criticality of resisting the urge to manage when what your team really needs is leadership. Finally, we discuss the most crucial role of leaders: cultivating a culture of accountability.

CHAPTER 10

BUILD AND ENABLE

*I firmly believe that any man's finest hour, the greatest
fulfillment of all that he holds dear, is that moment
when he has worked his heart out in a good cause
and lies exhausted on the field of battle—victorious.*

—Vince Lombardi, "What It Takes to Be Number One"

When you are the nucleus of an unconventional team that is trying to solve a big problem like cyberattacks on critical infrastructure [*or insert your particular big problem here*], you are the one who is coming up with all the ideas in the beginning. You are brainstorming with plank holders, you are recontextualizing the mission so that it can be conceptualized, and you are building out the necessary tools so that the fundamentals are clear and can easily be transferred to others as the team grows. All of that starts to melt away over time. Now, you are taking a step back as you go from being the lone wolf to becoming the team leader to the manager to the director to the VP. At that point, you are just there to provide visibility to people above you in the outside world, people like stockholders, board members, and politicians. You have built and enabled, you have focused on the basics, and you have given them all the tools they needed to succeed.

Most books about leadership and problem-solving center around The Leader. Those of us who sit at the top of the organizational structure have our egos stroked by proclaiming that our job is to be a "servant leader," which is a nice way of looking at it in theory, but in practice it is not well executed most of the time. Rather than being one who serves, I prefer to say that the leader's first job is to build and enable.

FROM DIGGING FOXHOLES
TO HANDING OUT TOOLS

The early stages of building and enabling look a lot different than they do on the back half. At first, you essentially have to do it all yourself. Recall Charlie Beckwith as he was founding Delta Force. How did he get the tools he needed to create his unit? He started by suiting up, getting into the arena, putting his head down, and DIYing it: doing guerilla operations in Malaysia with the British Special Air Service, catching a blood-borne infection in the jungles that very nearly killed him, and getting shot in the stomach with a .50 caliber machine gun in Vietnam. Through those experiences, he learned a different way of thinking about fighting and problem solving. He also learned what he did not like about the conventional military. He approached the U.S. Army with the idea of forming an unconventional SAS-style unit, but they were not interested. Undaunted, he continued to scrape and scratch for support for what he believed was the missing link to U.S. military dominance in the counterterrorism fight. He did not give up until he established Delta Force. He built it and then enabled it to grow and continue on without him.

That is what the unconventional team leader has to do. Basically, you start by picking up an entrenching tool (E-tool) and digging out a foxhole yourself until you figure out the most efficient techniques for digging. Then you grab another person, show them how to dig a trench, and take a step back. Now you have a visibility into that foxhole because you are standing above it, able to see the technique being used. You adjust; you refine the technique. You then snag another person who appears to have the right stuff and teach them the right way to dig. Once you have two foxholes done, you find another person and teach them how to teach others your way of digging foxholes. You grab a fourth one and teach that person how to teach someone to teach others who can then go out and do the work. You continue to do that time after time. The guys on the ground, the ones who are closest to the consequences for action and inaction, are now the ones who are making the decisions. That is building capability.

Once you are convinced that you have enough people to do the job, you work to ensure that they have enough E-tools and that you are putting them in the right places. That is the enablement piece. It all starts with a tactical microcosm. There is a saying that if I have six hours to chop down a tree, I'm going to spend the first four hours sharpening the axe. If I am told that I have two weeks to chop down the whole forest, I'm going to spend the first four hours sharpening the axe and figuring out the best technique to cut down a tree. The next four hours will be spent teaching five people how to show five other people each how to sharpen their axes and ultimately how to chop down trees in the most efficient manner.

The job of a leader is not to stand in front and charge up the hill. It is not to stand in back and tell people to go take the hill. It is to be whatever they need you to be to achieve the desired final outcome.

However, when you are trying to solve a problem as insidious and as rapidly evolving as cybersecurity, it is not only about teaching people how to wield E-tools or swing axes properly. That is part of it, of course. Most leaders teach people what to do and what to think and then stop there. Since the enemy has a vote, it is not enough to just teach your people what to do and think. That's the conventional approach. The unconventional team leader, once finished relaying the purely tactical techniques of digging holes and chopping trees, takes it a step further. This leader teaches people not *what* to think but *how to think strategically*, how to anticipate the actions of the adversary before they move. You learn that first yourself, just like you did when you were digging with the E-tool.

Instead of building a line of trenches, now you are building the trenches at an angle that makes it appear weak, ultimately drawing the enemy past those trenches (which were just there for show) and into your trap. Because you have done the reconnaissance, you know their tactics, techniques, and procedures. Once you have identified the weakness in their line, you attack that weak point with all your resources.

You do not win a war by following a prescribed formula that everyone, including your adversary, already knows. You win by teaching your team to think unconventionally and creatively, by teaching them how to break the rules. But first, you must have a full understanding of what is conventional.

SHAKING THINGS UP TO STRAIGHTEN THEM OUT

The surge in Iraq circa 2007 was effective not because a ton of additional resources were sent there. As pointed out earlier, the primary function of most of the troops there was to move logistics from one base to another. They were not going out and engaging the enemy because they were not very good at it. The enemy knew what their conventional approaches were and used that knowledge against them to deadly effect. We could have thrown all the convention in the world at our adversaries in Iraq and it would not have had a measurable impact. So, what did our military leaders do? They grabbed a couple of special operators and dropped them into infantry companies to work with a regular army captain and first sergeant to inject a new and unconventional way of thinking into their day-to-day activities. The operators were not there because they had better optics and could shoot faster. They were there to shake the infantry out of a rule-following mindset that bred complacency and limitation.

For instance, we had troops walking routes trying to get from Point A to Point B. On the way, they had come up against a fence line that, unbeknownst to them, was designed by the enemy to route them in the direction of a set of landmines. Our troops would walk along the fence line and BOOM. Extremely unfortunate and highly unnecessary. The boys taught them to think differently: *You do not have to follow the damn fences! Just pull out your wire cutters and open them up.* Now, instead of walking along the deadly route the enemy constructed for them, they could walk safely through the field. That simple shift in thinking interdicted the adversary before they could set things off—both literally in terms of their planted explosives and figuratively in terms of their overall battle plan—and, most importantly, protected the U.S. troops.

A similar thing happened in Mosul around 2008. The regular military were driving around during the day looking for bad guys and getting hit by IEDs. The enemy factions were causing traffic jams and throwing Russian armor-penetrating grenades at our troops while they were stuck in traffic. So, the other special operations elements tried to emulate our tactic of going out at night to get the enemy while they were sleeping, but eventually the enemy got wind of this and moved their encampments or positions. Every time our troops went out at night, they found a dry hole. Nobody was there. This happened for weeks until they finally called us.

We flew in from the west desert, where I was running ops, and started planning some new tactics. It was a conundrum. Again, the conventional wisdom had been not to go out during the day because you would get hit by IEDs, but then going out at night had not worked either. We decided to revert to going out in the middle of the day because that is when we knew we were effectively tracking the bad guys. Everybody looked at us like we were nuts. One of them said, "Really? You're the ones who taught us that going out at night was the best way to get these guys." And I replied, "Yeah, that was true until it wasn't."

By that point I had quite a lot of experience in Iraq. I had done six previous deployments there with two of my first three stints spent driving up and down the roads. The third deployment was the one in which I was hit by a bunch of IEDs. Because I had the most experience being on the road during the day, I was tapped to be the lead driver on these missions in addition to being the task force ops guy.

Keep in mind that we were supposed to be in Iraq to help the Iraqi people. We were not there to piss them off. Thus, the conventional rules of the road were that we were to follow traffic, drive the speed limit, not drive on the sidewalk, and so on. But following those largely "civilian" rules was putting us at risk. What did I do? I decided to break every rule for driving in Iraq. I drove fast—way faster than the conventional military was driving—and I never stopped until we got to our target.

One day we were driving down a road in Mosul that had three lanes of traffic on either side of a central median. Conventional wisdom dictated that we stay in the middle of the three lanes in case the enemy had planted IEDs in the median. On this particular day there was so much traffic, we were in danger of getting stuck and becoming sitting ducks for the Russian grenades or pulling up next to a vehicle-borne improvised explosive device (VBIED). So I decided to hop the median and straddle it, driving over it with my wheels on either side. Because my vehicle was so big, I hit every car on both sides of the median, but I did not stop. During the entire time we went after bad guys during the day (with a great deal of success in finding them, by the way) we only got hit by one IED, and it did not do any significant damage.

Regardless of our success in rooting out the enemies, there were some people in town who were not happy with my demolition derby approach to navigating the sunny streets of Mosul. Conventional military people, city leaders, and those types of folks were pretty upset. But as soon as it became clear that it was one of us behind the wheel, the outrage subsided quickly. After all, if it was a JSOTF guy driving like that, he must have had a good reason. That is how strong the JSOTF brand is.

For me, taking out the high-value targets that the other special operations group could not get was not the main reason I jumped that median and hit all those cars. It was also about protecting the asset. American taxpayers had spent millions of dollars finding, selecting, equipping, and training every one of the people on that mission. In my mind it was more important to keep our guys safe so they could do their jobs than it was to follow a set of questionable rules that the enemy could easily exploit. The rules were not made to hurt us intentionally, but that was the ultimate effect.

This is the pitfall of conventional wisdom and conventional approaches. Everything is novel at some point. Someone created the E-tool to enable troops en masse to dig trenches and foxholes without the logistical burden of moving loads of shovels. The E-tool allowed every soldier to carry their own and use it whenever needed, which occasionally included hand-to-hand combat with the enemy.

The difference I posit between building and enabling in the conventional versus the unconventional sense that I propose is simply this: Conventional wisdom builds policy, process, training, and tactics that enable large forces to do expected actions. The unconventional approach to building and enabling does all those things but generates an environment where the organization and the individuals that make it up have *tactical predictability*, *operational flexibility*, and *strategic efficiency*. This gives them license to adapt rapidly to changing needs and gives them a competitive advantage.

TACTICAL PREDICTABILITY

Tactical predictability is key. Take driving, for instance. Our approach to conveyance in America is based on an intricate system of predictable actions. You are supposed to drive on the right side of the road at the posted speed, stop at stop signs, stay within your lane, and use your turn signal. The government has a role in trying to control and enable this. They verify the basic understanding of the social compact (via written test) and functional ability under stress (every sixteen-year-old's driving test could easily be characterized as stressful). They occasionally fill potholes, put down painted stripes, set both speed limits and stop-light timing and duration, and they have a civil enforcement mechanism for rule following. Inevitably, humans—who largely do not understand *why* these "rules" exist—either blindly break them resulting in car crashes, struck bicyclists, traffic delays, and even fatalities, or blindly follow them (for example, sitting at a red light by yourself in the middle of the night with no cars in sight).

This was my issue with the Big Army as well as my experience working with conventional Marines early in my military career. As you may recall, I did not grow up with a particular fondness for people who believed they possessed ultimate authority. These military bosses' application of Alfred Lord Tennyson's description of the "Light Brigade"—"Theirs not to make reply, / Theirs not to reason why, / Theirs but to do and die"—in my opinion misses the point. In the military, most of your time is spent sitting around waiting for someone on high to tell you what to do. It is similar in the civilian world, but there, the order will probably come from some written standard operating procedure (SOP) or some snot-nose, first-line manager. If you ask why, they give you the consequence: "Because if you do not, you are fired," or "Because that's the way we do things here," or my personal favorite, "Because my boss said so."

This bastardizes the concept of tactical predictability in a completely understandable way. They need you to take out the trash because if clients see it, they will give a bad Yelp review, which will in turn hurt business and potentially result in the company losing money and having to lay you off. The garbage could also attract bugs, rats, and insects, potentially getting the business shut down by the health department. Same thing with the army or marines—if your unit is ordered to take a hill, there is an expectation that it will happen and there are other moving pieces that are dependent on that. For example, that hill may have enemy artillery batteries aimed over the waterway that will sink the landing craft that are critical to the turning of the war's tide.

To achieve tactical predictability, the rule is *do what you are told when you are told to do it* (a.k.a. compliance). The problem with following that rule is that it tends to repel the people you need the most—those with problem solving or special operations potential—and it builds the *superego* of everyone else. In Freudian psychology, the superego is the manifestation of your interactions with influential authority figures (typically parents, teachers, etc.), which is internalized as your moral conscience and deter-mines, sometime unwittingly, what you believe to be right or wrong.

What happens when *seeking understanding* becomes taboo? Well, the first line manager responds with consequence or hierarchical deferral (*the boss said so*) *because* they did not seek or expect to understand the why. You may have noticed that this book starts with *why* (and it is not because Simon Sinek is my idol, although I do respect his work) and ends with *leadership*. If you have a superego or culture at the individual contributor level that says *do what you are told, follow this list*, and so on, you are ensuring that the people who get promoted to first line manager will believe in that mantra. Thus, they will reward those who comply and admonish those who seek to understand. That means that the second level of management promoted in that same culture will now be managing their subordinates similarly, and so on and so forth, ultimately resulting in a conventional organization with limited capacity for impact. If, somehow, growing through the ranks of an organization endowed you with magical powers—perhaps the ability to suddenly seek clarity and be able to grasp the intricate dynamics of the problem you are solving, or the impact of your resources on it (as well as the ability to perfectly predict the ramifications of your adversaries, because remember: the enemy always gets a vote!)—then this rule to ensure tactical predictability would be just fine. But that is not how it works in real life most of the time.

The way we break the conventional rules of tactical predictability and become an elite problem-solving unit is by viewing our people less as round plastic objects on a checkerboard and more like an organism within an ecosystem. As an unconventional leader, you are in that ecosystem with them. They all have the ability to meet their individual and collective needs. They are expected to seek understanding, make decisions based on all the available information, and adapt to changing circumstances. The conventional rules are input, not prescription. At three in the morning, I am not going to sit at a red light for a minute when I know there are no cars coming from any direction at that hour. I also will not trust the drivers in South Florida to stay in their lanes or use a turn signal. The way that people tend to *break* the established order (the conventional rules) is also part of tactical predictability. This is another input that allows our nonconventional approach to work. We understand conventional rules, we understand conventional rule breaking, and we forge our nonconventional path in consideration of those data points.

Creating a competitive edge in the Fifth Domain is infinitely complex, as are other really challenging problems that are worthy of the focus and attention these techniques require. So how do we lead an approach that achieves tactical predictability and has an outsized impact? We start by *eliminating everything we do not need*. Right now, there is so much noise in the world of cybersecurity that it is impossible to wrap your mind around it—to grasp how broad and complexly nuanced the field presently is. Point solutions solve little, discrete problems but potentially create bigger problems when they are not strictly and universally applied (and continuously monitored)—open source this and API that. The products are numerous, the scope typically myopic, the acquisitions and subsequent shoddy integrations or implementations are myriad. Complexity is the enemy of security, so we add by subtracting or eliminating everything we do not need in order to reasonably manage the inputs we do need.

Complexity is also the enemy of progress in any domain. Remember: we are talking about the establishment of tactical predictability in an asymmetric environment. You can predict in CQB that your mate will turn left into the room unless the enemy or the layout of the room necessitates him turning right. He also knows if all the inputs are driving him right that the next guy will turn left. If you do not eliminate superfluous options then you will not be able to predict, and that is when gaps are created. As a leader, you have to not only build an ecosystem that allows people to understand the *why* but build a team that has seen the problems through the eyes of their teammates. When they are to a point of mastery, enable them to eliminate any unnecessary options, distractions, movements, or actions.

Simplification is similar. Assuming you get to a point at which you are eliminating the stuff you do not need so that everything you have or do is necessary (which is an ongoing process), you have to drive toward simplification. Many famous people have found wisdom in this concept.

Bill Gates has been credited with saying, "Always choose a lazy person to do a hard job because he will find the easiest way to do it." More seriously, as a leader in this approach, you cannot afford to have "lazy" people per se, but you can also not afford people who place a higher value on effort or activity than outcomes.

OPERATIONAL FLEXIBILITY

The conventional rule is that you reward people who do what they are told and put in extra effort. I have experienced this often as a business leader. Well intentioned managers or others will come to me saying things like, "These guys were up until 2:00 a.m. every night this week," or "This guy billed three hundred hours this month," or "I have taken on multiple roles." My response is always the same: *I appreciate the effort, but I reward outcomes.* The reality is that I have given them the operational flexibility to eliminate unnecessary actions and simplify the necessary ones. So, pulling an all-nighter should be followed by an intrinsic drive to simplify the process to preclude the error that led to the emergency in the first place. In sum, operational flexibility is the team's capability to respond to changes and uncertainty in the environment such that the mission is furthered and, ultimately, accomplished.

Moreover, operational flexibility is earned, not given. In *Team of Teams*, General Stan McChrystal talks about shared consciousness and empowered execution. For the lay reader, it is possible to come to the conclusion that "I was in the meeting, so I can make the decision." But that, like many other challenges associated with the fallacy of communication, is predicated on the notion that sharing information (telling someone) means that they heard, listened, comprehended, remembered, *and* made the appropriate adjustments to ensure that the desired outcome is achieved. In the military they even have different responses for these:

Copy = I heard you.

Roger = I understand.

Wilco = I understand and will comply.

As a leader, you have to build and enable your teams to achieve the operational flexibility to solve problems and stop walking past the dumpster fire. Much of this comes from brand, culture, selection, training, and so on, but the rest comes from their exposure to your leadership response.

Early in my tenure in special operations, I attended a training called Survival, Evasion, Resistance, and Escape (SERE) school. They forced a bag over my head, handcuffed me, and dragged me into a dark room where they forced me to squat. Loud foreign music was playing as my fellow captives were processed, stripped down, inspected, and placed in shoddy rags. The pain of squatting, the embarrassment, and the sensory deprivation were overwhelming. If someone made the mistake of sitting down, guards entered screaming, roughed them up, and left. I could not take it anymore. With legs burning, I sat. Guards came in and grabbed me. As they pulled me up, a massive hand came flying across my face, knocking me to the ground. I squatted. The guards left. I stayed there, toppling over and scrambling to get myself up quickly to avoid the punishment for failure to comply. Eventually, they came and got me. It was my turn to be shoved into "the box," a wooden container not big enough to stand in, but again we were not allowed to sit. The music was still blaring as guards were yelling at other boxes telling the occupants to get off the ground.

In reflection, it was only during the first thirty minutes of each phase that it was necessary for the guards to respond negatively to our natural response. That is all it took. For the rest of the time, most people—including the special operators I have referenced as being less likely to fall into these kinds of traps—self-policed. It reminds me of how animal trainers chain young elephants to big trees to be able to control them when they are larger. The little elephants will try to break free for a while, but they quickly learn that they cannot. By the time the animals have grown big enough to yank a tree up by the roots and liberate themselves with ease, they will not even try. Thus, thereafter, a seven-ton elephant can be chained to a little stake stuck in the ground and he will stand there forever. You see, leaders of all stripes (including parents) tend to act like SERE school guards and elephant trainers, which leads to the development of a superego that kills operational flexibility, even with the best of intentions.

STRATEGIC EFFICIENCY

Given that operational flexibility must be earned and a negative response to instinctual operational flexibility kills it in the long term, how do you build and enable the operational flexibility required to achieve strategic efficiency?

The conventional answer is to hire an expert who has the right knowledge, skills, and abilities (KSAs) or Executive Core Qualifications (ECQ). After all, they are the ones with demonstrated success in your industry, right? Here is the problem with that, though: They have not solved the problem yet. You do not hire conventional military commanders into special operations units (although you do see leaders like General Stan McChrystal and General Austin "Scott" Miller take over major conventional efforts).

BREAK THIS RULE:

To enable operational flexibility
and achieve strategic efficiency,
hire industry experts.

BREAK THIS RULE:

Hire people who do what they are
told when they are told to do it; in
other words, hire compliers.

With the approach we are talking about, everyone needs to be the FNG or 6IC,[19] regardless of their background and experience. They have to be on a small team in which their team leader (title irrelevant) has earned the operational flexibility and is able to see the outcome in terms of strategic efficiency.

A quotation attributed to Steve Jobs states, "I noticed that the dynamic range between what an average person could accomplish and what the best person could accomplish was fifty or one hundred to one. Given that, you are well advised to go after the cream of the cream. A small team of A-plus players can run circles around a giant team of B and C players." Your job is the build and enable that process to happen, not to manage the resources that are making it happen.

---

19   In military parlance, FNG = fucking new guy, and 6IC = sixth in charge.

CHAPTER 11

FIGHT THE URGE
TO MANAGE

A good [leader] trains and delegates . . . and you can't do that if you're taking on everything—regardless of how important the task is—yourself.

—**Karen Dillon,** quoted in Rebecca Knight,
"How to Stop Micromanaging Your Team"

nce you have scaled out to where the mission and the team are self-replicating in the manner of a virus, it is not possible to control everything anymore. Your span of tactical control is minute by this stage, and now you have managers overseeing the day-to-day operations and providing tactical direction. It is at this point that you have to fight the urge to manage.

Since the manager is the one who is going to be abruptly awakened at two in the morning as a consequence of their decisions, you want them to be the one calling the shots. Trying to keep your thumb on everything at this stage is like putting a shark in a fishbowl. The shark can control all that is going on in there, but it is never going to grow past six inches.

Eventually, it is going to starve unless somebody feeds it. But if you put a shark in the ocean, it grows to twenty feet long pretty quickly. Now the ocean is a much more vibrant ecosystem, allowing the shark to have a much larger impact.

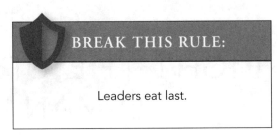

BREAK THIS RULE:

Leaders eat last.

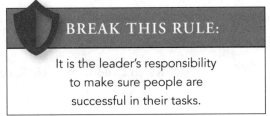

BREAK THIS RULE:

It is the leader's responsibility to make sure people are successful in their tasks.

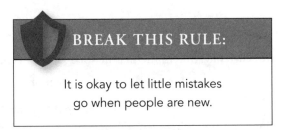

BREAK THIS RULE:

It is okay to let little mistakes go when people are new.

Thus, your job as the leader shifts from managing everything in your universe to providing the necessary tools and appropriate protections for those who are making decisions. Only then can you give this ecosystem that is solving a large, complex problem the necessary authority and power to be able to execute the mission. Now you can have a broad, sweeping impact.

I recognize that stepping back and delegating authority is a major challenge for some people, especially those who do not know the difference between leadership and management. Those are two very different ways of operating. Leadership is creating a thriving ecosystem, whereas management is directing the necessary activities for a task to be completed within that ecosystem.

Fighting that urge to manage and allowing the shins to get scraped (while simultaneously preventing the necks from being broken) is a lot like being a parent. If you hover over your kid and hold the bike so they never fall, they are never going to realize how to maintain their own equilibrium. At the same time, you do not throw a seven-year-old on a motorcycle because they could smash into a wall and now you have failed. You give them just enough to get going but not enough to get done. At first, the right people on your team will see the gap or error and judge accordingly. The wrong people won't correct or improve. *Eventually the wrong people will be exposed, and the right people will realize why and integrate it into their own leadership style.* It takes strength and fortitude to keep your mouth shut and let your best new teammates believe—even briefly—that you know less than you actually do, or that you are not as capable as you are in fact. It is critical for evaluation as much as it is critical to ensuring you that you are leveraging the full capacity of the organization. Fighting the urge to manage helps you determine whether your people care about getting the job done, care about avoiding the social implications of being wrong, or are okay with doing something that does not make sense because they are not responsible. As a leader, you have to let the organization be both self-selecting and self-improving.

THE DIRTY DISHES DILEMMA

It has been my experience that in every domestic relationship, the couple at some point runs into the Dirty Dishes Dilemma. The dilemma goes something like this: Boyfriend hastily throws the dishes in the dishwasher. Girlfriend opens the dishwasher to find dishes with seemingly permanent caked-on food. The silverware is intermingled and tangled, which increases the degree of difficulty associated with unloading and putting it away (assuming that any of the utensils are actually clean). Girlfriend has a few options here: (1) do not say anything and just rewash them herself, (2) tell Boyfriend she will just do the dishes from now on, (3) get mad and write and post an SOP, or (4) show him how to wash them to her satisfaction and ensure he knows that using that approach will be viewed positively. Let us review the likely outcomes of each:

- Option 1: Boyfriend will believe he is *helping*, so if Girlfriend ever corrects him in the future (which, come on, you know she will), it will cause a significant emotional event. Basically, she will be changing the standard procedures after they have been codified.

- Option 2 gives Boyfriend an out. Girlfriend will be doing those dishes for as long as the couple is together and will eventually get to a point where her disdain for his "laziness" detracts from the relationship—even though it is *all her fault*.

- Option 3 is management. It can work, but the practical dynamic will always be "because she told me so" and not "because this is what we need to do to stay healthy and maintain our household ecosystem." He will then very likely walk past any household task that lacks an SOP because they are not acting as a team—she is acting like his mom.

- Option 4 is leadership. I guarantee Boyfriend will either create or adopt a more effective dishwasher-stacking strategy or go out and buy a space-age dishwasher that cleans the dishes for him without having to rinse them in advance. Refer back to what Bill Gates said; Boyfriend isn't necessarily lazy, but he is most likely to help the household achieve strategic efficiency because he is closest to the consequence.

How a couple or a team responds to the Dirty Dishes Dilemma is a life sentence (or at least for the life of that relationship or that team). People do not rise to the level of expectation or ability. They fall to the level of their training. If they are properly selected, understand the desired outcome, are properly trained and empowered with operational flexibility, they will generate far more strategic efficiency over time than even the most well-crafted SOP.

CHAPTER 12

ACCOUNTABILITY

We view ourselves on the eve of battle. We are nerved for the conquest and must conquer or perish. It is vain to look for present aid: None is at hand. We must now act or abandon all hope!

—**General Sam Houston,** "To the People of Texas"

Each time our unit returned from combat, we entered a period of lower-level activities for a few months while we recuperated and waited for our next deployment. During this time, we would do team trips, trainings, and other exercises designed to keep us sharp. There is one particular training that comes to mind whenever I think of the subject of this chapter on accountability. It was a training with live chemical warfare agents, and it consisted of reconnaissance, ion mobility spectroscopy to identify the type and location of threat agents, munitions identification, sensitive site exploitation/evidence collection, facility destruction (evaluating and implementing techniques to prevent future use), sampling, medical training, decontamination, and evidence chain-of-custody.

In preparation for this event, one of my teammates (I call him "Dick" for a reason that is about to become obvious) was put in charge of gathering and packing our gear into the shipping containers to be sent to the training location. Our protective suits, masks, filters, gloves, booties, the decontamination equipment—Dick was responsible for loading it all up and shipping it off. We arrived at the training location on the appointed day and started to suit up for our exercise, only to discover that Dick had packed the wrong batteries for our powered air purifying respirators. Those batteries were a force multiplier; they were not absolutely necessary for us to do the mission, but they certainly would have made us a lot more comfortable inside our massive rubbery protective suits in scorching hot weather. Having powered air respirators in that situation is like having an air conditioner blowing on your face, whereas not having them is like trying to suck fresh air through a six-foot straw: extremely difficult, physically exhausting, and highly unpleasant.

Since our trainers were always on the lookout for teachable moments, they decided that we would go forward with the training without the powered respirators to reinforce the lessons that (a) you have to adjust to the unexpected, (b) you have to continually test your grit, and (c) that the lapse of one teammate—one Dick, if you will—negatively affects everyone. The fact that this one guy forgot the batteries resulted in everybody participating in the training event having to suffer unnecessarily. Consequently, our effectiveness as a unit was reduced. Dick was held accountable; he was fired for his mistake.

The critically important lesson is that when it comes to accountability, dead is dead.

This is why I saved the topic of accountability for last—because it is potentially the most important leadership activity there is. Providing consequences, both positive and negative, becomes the central focus of leadership once you have empowered the people on the ground to make the decisions.

BREAK THIS RULE:

Acknowledging people's
effort builds morale.

Here is the way I look at it in my own company: I am growing a cybersecurity toolset, building software. I am looking at or for the mechanisms to enable compliance, maturity, and effectiveness to be as easy and scalable as possible regardless of the level of the organization or adversary. I am giving the people on my team the tools and the training to be able to eliminate, simplify, and automate everything. As we scale, I cannot control the development of that software because it has to be continually evolving and adapting to changes in the operational environment. So I empower people in the company who are closest to the consequences to do whatever they need to do to get that job done. If the person in charge of that effort ultimately makes a bad call that causes a massive outage or enables a back door, I have to be there to protect the entity and provide top cover, and also to dish out consequences to those responsible for the negative effect.

Alternatively, when team members do great things, I have to be there to provide mechanisms that reward them based on what they care about. Not everybody is motivated by money; not everybody is motivated by more time off. Some of them want to be rewarded by being able to do cooler stuff or being involved in more sophisticated exploration. My job is to figure that out and implement it. Thus, accountability is the primary responsibility of leaders of unconventional teams like mine. It is not my job to direct all the actions and bear all the consequences myself, because that approach mitigates the reach that we can achieve when trying to solve something as prolific and ubiquitous as global war in the Fifth Domain.

Having said all that, there is more to accountability than leaders standing over people and cracking whips at them when they mess up or making it rain when they do well. That is the conventional approach, and you know how I feel about that. No, there is a type of accountability that's practically unassailable—a level of accountability that you can begin fostering and reinforcing in your organization today that will turn your team into a force of nature. Actually, by doing the things I've recommended in this book to build an elite team, you will already have laid the groundwork for this form of accountability—*cultural accountability*—to take root and grow. But before we get into that, let's look at the two more common and conventional types of accountability—*personal* and *hierarchical*—and consider the effects of each on the unconventional team.

PERSONAL AND HIERARCHICAL ACCOUNTABILITY

In Chapter 10, I touch on the Freudian concept of the superego and how it can diminish a person's problem-solving capability. Freud also identified the id—the deep, primitive, instinctual, unconscious side of your personality—and the ego, that part of the id that has been influenced by the rules of the outside world. And again, the superego is like your conscience—how you were trained by your parents or other authority figures to behave in certain ways within the mores of society.

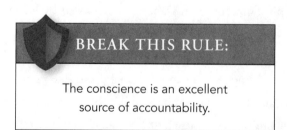

BREAK THIS RULE:

The conscience is an excellent source of accountability.

Personal accountability is your alignment to that superego. You know you *should* do something, so you do it. It is waking up at five in the morning and going to the gym even though you would rather sleep in, or studying for a test even though you would rather join your friends for happy hour, or showing up to work on time when nobody is checking. Respect your elders, never throw the first punch—those kinds of societal norms. Most people would define it as integrity.

So yes, personal accountability is a good thing to have, but it is not the predominant kind of accountability you want on your team when you are trying to fight an asymmetrical war. First, personal accountability is about adhering to whatever construct an individual has, and most of those constructs are conventional, having been pounded into them by authority figures. Most people are brought up to *follow* the rules, not *break* them; they are taught to stick with conventional wisdom, not toss it out the window. Following rules and clinging to conventional wisdom are not how we win a David versus Goliath fight.

Second, navigating the world guided solely by personal accountability tends to set people up for "othering," which, as discussed in an earlier chapter, makes it hard (if not impossible) to see the world through the adversary's eyes in order to anticipate their next move. If you and your teammates cannot do that—if your strict adherence to your personal definitions of "crazy" and "sane" and "good" and "evil" prevent you from understanding your adversary—then you cannot beat them, no matter how much you may wish to do so.

Third, there is no metric for personal accountability when one is engaged in warfare or other asymmetrical fights. Personal accountability does not kick in during these scenarios because there is no foundation of the superego around engaging with the enemy. In the vast majority of cases, your parents and religious leaders never taught you that. You do not have personal accountability as an option when you are involved in situations like this, scenarios you have never been in before, that nobody ever expected you to be in. Most people have no frame of reference for it.

Hierarchical accountability means that you behave in certain ways because if you do not, there will be negative consequences. You show up to work on time because your boss is watching to see when you clock in, and if you are late, he is going to be on your back. You turn in the homework so your parents will not get a nasty note from the teacher and ground you. You are not acting out of passion or a desire to do what is right. You are only trying to avoid creating a problem for yourself. Even if the people on your team have both personal and hierarchical accountability, they will only do what they think is right. However, once they believe they have satisfied that benchmark, they will tend to do only what they believe they are going to be held accountable for—no more, no less.

The trouble with hierarchical accountability in a team that is fighting a complex problem is that (a) there's no metric for hierarchical accountability when you are solving these types of problems, and (b) the "generals" are not even around when the decisions are being made. The powers that be are not going to come swooping in to analyze your tactics, point out your mistakes, set you straight—at least not until it is far too late.

The traditional norms of personal and hierarchical accountability are not enough when you are operating in this world, solving these really hard problems, and breaking all the rules. Those two types of accountability diminish a team's ability to adapt to changing circumstances and lead to a lower expectation of individual and team performance. They do not enable you to make the best risk-based decisions through which you can take artistic liberty, such as determining where you need to put additional focus to make the most efficient, positive impact. For an organization to do that consistently requires *cultural accountability.*

CULTURAL ACCOUNTABILITY

When I was in special operations, all the missions we went on were about going after high-value targets. Most of the missions involved doing what is called "attacking the network" to gain access into any point in the target's web of associates. Recall how they got Osama bin Laden by identifying his courier, following him around, tracking where he went, and seeing who he interacted with. By doing that, you establish a pattern of life that further illuminates the network. The intention is to build this spiderweb of contacts that generates access and placement. This access and placement enables you to gain both an understanding of the organizational structure and methods of access. With that you can identify the right method to access the high-value targets that you want to take out.

This was what we had been doing for weeks during one particular mission in Iraq. We tracked a network connected to VBIED attacks until we finally narrowed down the location of our main target. We expected that there would be explosives and foreign fighters all around this guy. At that stage of the campaign, and given the characteristics of the target, we had to decide: Do we fly directly into the target, or do we land offsite and sneak in? Do we access the doors and hit it from the roof and the ground at the same time? Do we surround the place and have an interpreter on a loudspeaker telling them to come out with their hands up? Or do we just drop a bomb on the joint?

This was one of those scenarios in which, because of the probability that there were foreign fighters with suicide vests and women and children inside, we chose to hit the target hard and fast rather than do a call out or a bombing. Following the principles of speed, surprise, and violence of action, we were going to blow the doors, enter the house, and engage the enemy in CQB to try and minimize collateral damage. We would take out all military-aged males who had weapons and avoid hitting the women and kids.

On the appointed night, we burst into the first room of this house to find a terrorist with an AK-47. One of my mates (I will call him Vince) attempted to fire on that guy, but his weapon jammed. Vince immediately transitioned to his secondary weapon and took a shot.

Now, let me explain something before I tell you what happened next. Many people think that when someone gets shot, they are dead. Not necessarily true. Much depends on *where* they are shot. In special operations we are trained to aim for the A-zone—a small section of the chest right above the sternum—because a shot there damages the bad guy's central nervous system such that they cannot hold a gun anymore, let alone pull a trigger. If you hit someone in the arm or leg, they will most likely stay alive for a while—it takes a long time to bleed out from the average extremity wound—and an armed bad guy with that kind of superficial injury can do a lot of damage to you and your partners in a matter of seconds. That is why we are trained to hit the A-zone.

Back to the mission: After Vince's gun jammed, he pulled his pistol and shot the terrorist, not in the A-zone but in the shoulder. Immediately thereafter he fired another round that hit the terrorist in the A-zone. Lights out. Good outcome for everyone but the terrorist. We got the rest of the bad guys (four of them), safely removed six women and children, did the site exploitation, and gathered the intel, whereupon the helicopters came to pick us up.

At the conclusion of every mission, the team would meet to discuss and learn from what had just transpired. What had gone right, what had gone wrong, and everything in between. At the meeting after this particular mission, Vince acknowledged that his primary weapon had jammed, he had pulled out his pistol, and he had put the first shot in the shoulder and the second in the A-zone. That was it. That was all that was said by him or anyone else about that aspect of the day's work.

After that deployment, we returned to the States, and every morning for the next six months, when I drove to work at the base, I saw Vince doing target practice at the range. First thing every single morning, rain or shine. I knew why he was out there. To him, that first shot to the shoulder was a miss, and he was going to make damn sure it never happened again. Even though the action was successful in the end, it was not executed perfectly. We did not have to point that out to Vince. He knew. He fully understood on his own that the consequences could have been catastrophic for us all had the bad guy been able to return fire. Nobody told him to do target practice every day for six months. Nobody was checking on him to make sure he did it. He just did it, day after day after day, because that is the kind of dedication and responsibility that is expected in our SMU, and he was not going to let us down.

That is the power of cultural accountability.

Cultural accountability is vastly different from the personal and hierarchical kinds because it is totally voluntary and proactive. It is not imposed by parents or bosses. It comes straight from the heart and the gut and the disciplined intellect. Building and enabling that type of accountability in an organization requires a different process from the other two forms, but it is pretty straightforward. *It's the natural by-product of building and enabling an elite, self-selecting team that is doing cool things that make an impact with people they like.*

This is the type of thing you do not see just anywhere: a team of folks who have complete openness and clarity around what they are doing right, what they are doing wrong, and what needs to change, all without finger-pointing and blame-gaming. Even though they do not have all the details about the asymmetrical problem they are trying to solve on this rapidly changing battlefield, they know where they are headed. They are "on purpose" at all times. They do not sit around waiting for the brass to give them their marching orders every morning. They suit up and go. They are a group of individuals taking extreme ownership in making adjustments to the battle plan as they move forward, bolstered by the confidence that they have permission to break the rules of convention if that is what it takes to defeat their Goliath—and that most certainly *is* what it is going to take.

ACKNOWLEDGMENTS

To the kids: I hope someday you will read this and understand. You inspire me every day, and I will never stop fighting to protect your ability to chart your own path, find your purpose, and explore the art of the possible. The sound of the guns may draw and focus my attention, but even when I am away from you mentally or physically, you are always with me.

To the special operations community past and present: My words cannot express the gratitude I feel for the sacrifices you make on our behalf. Perilous and complex global operations—some acknowledged but most not—that have an outsized impact on our world and give kids like me both the inspiration and opportunity to reject our lot in life and accomplish so much more.

To my mates: You gave me the opportunity over and over again to be in the thick of things. The lessons I learned from you have been my true north in taking on this new domain of warfare. I consider my time with you to have been formative. Though my time before and after you might demonstrate some examples of what not to do, you showed me what right looks like.

To those who gave me a chance when other people would not, sometimes through a seemingly small decision or kindness: Without you I would probably be stuck somewhere in the mountain laurel of life instead of at my next RV. In no particular order, I thank you:

Pat: To this day I do not know why, but you seemed to always be there when I needed a chance—from my first selection to my last and countless missions in between. I know I did not always make the most of those opportunities at the time, but without the experience they afforded, I would not be who I am today.

Tim: No one I have ever met has been a better example of a true leader. Whenever I am torn on how to move forward or handle a situation, the example you set guides me through it.

Matt: From the moment you pulled the dollar out of your sock at the end of "I" phase to saving my ass from sleeping through pick-up, you have been one of the best friends in my life. The sacrifices you, Paula, and the kids have made over all these years, not just in the fight but at the sharpest tip of the spear, are so far beyond what could ever be asked, expected, or accomplished by any but the finest warriors.

Gerard: Very few are cut from your cloth, seeing through the pain of practical application of power, precision, and speed applied by an emotionless opponent as inspiration. You saw something others refused to and rescued me from an unbalanced life in which I was doing cool stuff that made an impact but not with people I liked. You believed in me and what we could do together when nobody else would. You have given me, for the first time since I left the unit, a sense of belonging, as well as the runway to build something truly special.

To the men and women of Conquest: You make it happen every day, learning, building, progressing, and adapting on the front lines of this war, engaged with determined and sophisticated adversaries. What you do is critical to protecting our way of life.

Last, I thank those who helped make this book happen. Henry and Gerard: I know this seemed like a strange and potentially unnecessary activity in the midst of running a rapidly growing business, but you supported it anyway. I hope it exceeded your expectations. Pamela, Jody, and Carmen: Thank you for the countless hours of effort, discussion, coordination, and organization. Without you, this would have taken another lifetime to complete.

APPENDIX

BE WILLING TO BREAK THESE RULES TO STACK THE DECK

The following is a list of the top "rules" that we have to break to gain a competitive edge in cyber. Each is followed by a brief explanation of why breaking the rule is often so critical to success.

RULE: Buy the best-of-breed technologies.
REALITY: Most investments never get properly implemented and fail to integrate.

RULE: It is only war if tanks are in the street.
REALITY: If we do not mobilize, we will lose the deterrence impact of our competitive advantage and end up with tanks in the streets.

RULE: We should only worry about the barbarians at the gate.
REALITY: Our current and future adversaries are quietly infiltrating from far-away, remote locations.

RULE: Never throw the first punch.

REALITY: All it takes is one. If you cannot avoid a fight (most of the time, you can) then you should hit first and hit hard. Being well trained is a major contributor to avoidance.

RULE: The government will protect us from the really bad guys.

REALITY: The attack surface is too big, and there are too many soft targets to protect.

RULE: Leaders should treat everyone the same.

REALITY: Everyone has different needs, skills, and aspirations. They are not robots.

RULE: Being elite or exclusive limits diversity and is unfair.

REALITY: Being elite requires diversity of background, experiences, innovativeness, and thought.

RULE: Put people in the role they are best suited for and get out of their way.

REALITY: You have to challenge people to understand their limits and encourage growth.

RULE: Leaders eat last.

REALITY: Leaders ensure that the logistics are in place to ensure that everyone gets fed and they eat when they can.

RULE: Soften your feedback to avoid discouraging people.

REALITY: If you do not provide clarity, then the behavior will not get corrected. As my professor says, "If you don't straighten them out, they will be crooked forever."

RULE: Acknowledging people's effort builds morale.

REALITY: Effort is always secondary to outcome.

ABOUT THE AUTHOR

Whether he is protecting his platoon from ambush on a dusty road outside Baghdad as a young army sergeant, taking out high-value terrorist targets as a member of the elite special operations community, crushing a jiujitsu opponent to win a Pan-American Championship title, or strategizing about how to block hackers from attacking critical American infrastructure systems, Jeffrey J. Engle's fighting style is best characterized as *unconventional*. Cool. Calculated. Gritty. And totally disconcerting to his adversaries.

As the chairman and president of Conquest Cyber, headquartered in Miramar, Florida, Engle leads a nimble team of security analysts helping the defense industry and health care and finance companies build resilient cybersecurity programs that protect the American way of life. But to Engle, where he is today is not nearly as important as where he has been.

Growing up amid poverty and homelessness, ten-year-old Engle and his siblings were kidnapped from their father by their mother, who used them to commit welfare fraud, eventually abandoning them in a California crack house. Engle attended twenty different schools during his childhood before ultimately being reunited with other family members. Inspired by his beloved paternal grandfather—a veteran of World War II, the Korean War, and the Vietnam War—seventeen-year-old Engle talked his father into signing an age waiver so he could join the army. He would spend the next several years in combat zones, deployed during Operation Enduring Freedom and Operation Iraqi Freedom.

Engle would go on to earn two Bronze Star Medals, the Purple Heart, the Meritorious Service Medal, the Army Commendation Medal for Valor, the Combat Action Badge, and the Military Freefall Parachutists Badge in addition to being selected as one of the youngest members of the world's most elite fighting unit. He considers his time in special operations to be his formative years, when he learned how to do things right and adopted an unconventional approach to solving the toughest of challenges, including the pursuit and elimination of several of the highest-value targets in the war on terror.

Following his medical retirement from special operations, Engle continued his fight to protect the country that gave him the opportunity to thrive despite his childhood challenges. Through his work with the Defense Threat Reduction Agency, he oversaw emergency management and mass warning/notification systems following terrorist attacks, school shootings, and the like. He devised and coordinated training exercises at the national level to prepare for attacks with weapons of mass destruction and responded to the Ebola outbreak in Sierra Leone, writing a book on disease emergence in the Asia-Pacific region.

Engle was then tapped to create and lead Conquest Cyber to help protect critical American assets from ongoing cyberattacks using the philosophies and tactics he learned in special ops. A graduate of Virginia Tech, where he earned a master's degree in political science, Engle has also earned a cybersecurity certificate from Harvard University. His hobbies include flying, diving, and deep-sea fishing.